When Feelings Don't Come Easy

Overcoming the struggles to feel good about your LIFE!

By
Craig A. Miller

AmErica House
Baltimore

First printing

ISBN: 1-58851-581-8
PUBLISHED BY AMERICA HOUSE BOOK PUBLISHERS
www.publishamerica.com
Baltimore

Printed in the United States of America

TABLE OF CONTENTS

Preface

I. Why feelings don't come easy

II. Find healing through your feelings!

Preface

In the people helping profession, I have always learned that expressing feelings through words and tears is a major source of release from inner hurts. This release aids in the healing process. When I was training in graduate school I was repeatedly reminded to ask the question, "And how does that make you feel?" to help clients release inner emotions. For many therapists today this is still the standard question of choice.

Ironically, it has been my experience over the years that this question has brought more confusion, frustration, and silence than any other question. For many people, the process of trying to identify and appropriately express feelings about a past situation becomes a difficult and frustrating experience. For others, feelings are avoided since they may represent the reliving of pain, fears, or trauma that are buried inside. Or, feelings may be avoided because they may bring a sense of being helpless or out of control. Still others have pushed away feelings for so long they become emotionless to situations around them. It became more obvious that the very question I thought was going to help release feelings, often made people feel worse. It doesn't make sense to expect people to readily release feelings if they cannot identify them or are afraid to let them out.

It became clear that one of the most common but subtly devastating problems affecting people with hurting pasts is the difficulty in identifying inner emotions. At the heart of a fragile self- worth, dissatisfaction with life, dysfunctional relationships, and emotional or physical illness lies the inability to identify and effectively communicate feelings. In our lifelong quest to find purpose and meaning for our lives, there is the need to express our God-given feelings. This expression helps us find significance in ourselves, in our relationships, and in the truth of everyday experiences.

Without meaningful expressions of our inner feelings, we will be unsuccessful in satisfying our own needs and the needs of others. For example, our ability to give love and receive love from another person (including God) has everything to do with how we learned (or did not learn) to identify and express inner feelings. This is experienced to a greater extent in difficulty in developing and maintaining meaningful relationships and getting our needs met in those relationships. Among the many reasons for the national divorce rate of over fifty percent for first-time marriages and close to seventy-five percent for second-time marriages is the lack of meaningful communication between partners. Most couples do not know how to interpret their own feelings, let alone respect the feelings of their spouse.

This book represents over twenty-two years of listening to hurting people with stories of confusion, frustration, pain, and suffering. To help you apply this to your own life, individual case examples were developed by combining many of the stories heard over the years. The names picked for each case example are fictitious. These examples were developed from the type of issues heard over and over again that I believed would best emphasize the fact that you are not alone in your daily struggles and desire for healing.

God gave you feelings as a standard part of your daily operating equipment. But unhealthy relationships may have robbed you of your ability to express those feelings. God wants you to let go of the hurts accumulated throughout life and become free to feel the peace and joy life has to offer. In order to accomplish this, you need to get back to the basic understanding of what God intended you to feel and allow His truth to set you free. Over and over again I have witnessed people freed from the bondage of emotional suffering, physical illness, relationship difficulties, and a host of other problems that repeatedly plagued their daily existence. The conception of the techniques found in this book began in the early 1990's with many refinements over the years. These techniques have been time-tested and become highly effective in empowering people to make the needed changes in their own lives.

I have witnessed the power of prayer, faith, and God's wisdom as effective tools used toward the goal of healing. When I began using these tools in helping people, not only did I find my therapeutic abilities enhanced, but people were coping better and becoming healed from their sufferings in a shorter amount of time than originally expected. The blessing is that these tools are free to anyone who chooses to use them. As a result, I am forever grateful to Jesus Christ for the wisdom and guidance He has given me toward my passion to help the hurting people who enter my life.

I am also grateful to my loving wife Marilyn and our two children, Brian and Paul, for their patience and support during the writing of this book. In addition, I am grateful to Pastor and author Clark Cothern for his prayers and helpful guidance during the conception of this book. I also greatly appreciate the prayerful support and words of encouragement of Katie Hiatt and Becky Cunningham. Lastly, I am grateful to AmErica House for allowing this book to be published.

It is my prayer that this book will be the vessel to begin the healing process for you and thousands more who are searching to find the truth about themselves and freely experience the love, peace, and joy that everyone deserves. Let the healing begin in you!

I

Why feelings don't come easy

Chapter 1

What is so important about expressing your feelings?

May the words of my mouth and the meditation
of my heart be pleasing in your sight, O Lord,
my Rock and my Redeemer
(Psalm 19:14)

Jane came into my office with a look of despair on her face. She explained, "It's like I have all these feelings going on inside, but I don't know what to say." I encouraged her to describe what goes on inside when she is with her family or during work situations. "I have no joy in my life, like a dark cloud is over my head and I cannot get rid of it," she said. "I'm in a good mood one minute and then a bad mood the next. If someone starts arguing I just want to leave the room," she said while looking at the floor. Jane found it difficult to be with other people when they were upset. She frequently judged herself, always wondering if she was making the right decision. Jane strived to do a good job as a wife and mother but struggled with thoughts that it was not good enough. She found it hard to say "no" to people, leaving little time for her to enjoy activities. She was tired of putting on a smiley face when she felt empty inside. She acknowledged having these feelings for many years but felt helpless to do anything about them.

Jane said the relationship with her parents was "good," but acknowledged she did not always feel emotionally close to them. She did not often see her parents show or communicate emotions, and emotions were not always encouraged with other members of the family. Jane remembered an occasional kiss from her mother, but had few memories where she felt emotionally close. Her father was often away from home and considered emotionally distant. Jane recalled how her parents' frequent arguing resulted in many types of confusing feelings. When Jane became angry or cried, she was either sent to her room or she would go there to get away from her parents' comments. Her room was a safe place to avoid conflict in the family.

Jane described herself as always striving to meet her parent's expectations. Since her parents did not provide much approval for accomplishments, Jane found herself frequently trying to find approval through her activities such as helping around the house. Even though she tried to do her best, one of the parents would often have some type of negative comment. This contributed to the belief deep inside that she was not good enough and needed to work harder to please everyone. If something happened around the house Jane would be questioned, making her believe she was somehow to blame. She learned to keep peace in the family at all costs – even at the cost of not being honest with herself about what she felt inside. Not allowing herself to feel became a way of life. This was especially true to avoid anything that resembled approaching conflict with those around her.

Her overwhelming need to find approval many times motivated her beyond her emotional or physical strength. This was evident when she would finish everyone's projects, believing that completing the work on her own was easier than having to deal with the conflict from asking others to be responsible for themselves. Jane never liked the feeling of anxiety that would accompany any type of conflict with others. When someone confronted her she would either want to change the subject or leave the room. When she became upset, she found cleaning the house was the best way to keep her mind off her feelings.

Jane also realized she simply did not know how to identify and express what was going on inside of her mind and body. Holding in feelings all her life was physically and mentally taking its toll. Her accumulation of hurts and pain were evident in her frequent mood swings, anxiety, and lack of joy in her life. She complained of frequent stress headaches, fatigue, and a lack of motivation to be involved with social activities. It was as if her body and mind were screaming out for help, telling her to let out her feelings, but Jane admitted she did not know how.

Struggling with the ups and downs of life

Have you ever had struggles like Jane? Do your moods frequently slide up and down, like a sunny day one minute and a cloudy day the next? Is your life empty, with a dark cloud hanging over your head? Do you often become overwhelmed inside with feelings of nervousness, fear, hurt, anger, disappointment, jealousy, guilt, sadness, helplessness, or hopelessness? In stressful situations do you want to hide or explode, or feel short of breath or numb all over? Do you struggle with finding words to describe what is going on inside or do you find yourself not able to feel anything at all? No matter how hard you try to do things right, is it a battle to feel good about what you do? Has life been like an uphill battle, wondering when you will reach the top – only to find occasional rest stops along the way? Are you tired of looking for answers, believing this is the way life has to be? Do you wish you could find the truth behind this life of misery, desiring to take control of your life?

If these struggles are describing what you are experiencing, you are not alone. In my counseling office I regularly hear the familiar stories of inner turmoil from men and women who have difficulty finding joy and happiness in their life. This is the struggle for people who cannot identify and express what they feel. You become helpless to the difficulty of identifying what is happening inside. You struggle with getting your needs and desires met because you cannot express what you feel. Your mind is bursting with emotion, but you either stuff them away because you cannot feel or let it out in explosions of words or behaviors you regret later. For example, when you get into situations of conflict, you may become afraid, angry, or nervous – wanting to get away. You may freeze up, finding difficulty in saying what is on your mind or you blurt out some hurtful words after you cannot take it any longer. You later wonder why you behaved that way, not liking yourself for what you did. You tell yourself you want to change, but end up repeating the same behaviors. Since no answers can be found, you reluctantly assume that life is destined to be like a roller coaster ride of inner struggles.

If you have the thinking that life must be a struggle with no sense of joy, you are living a lie. You do not need to constantly live with fear, anxiety, anger, guilt, sadness, hopelessness, helplessness, or any other overwhelming feelings. You need to learn how to control those feelings, rather than allow them to control you. One reason why you have not changed is because no one has told you why you react the way you do and what to do when you have those feelings. How you learned to identify and express feelings as a child impacts how you will live with feelings as an adult. If you do not freely express your feelings as an adult, you are destined to live a life of emotional dysfunction and misery. To make the greatest change in your life, let us begin the process of exploring what is so important about expressing your feelings.

Feelings are outward messages from the heart

God created you with feelings as a natural way to tell others of your innermost desires, needs, and reactions to what is happening. If you look at a baby you will see the most basic example of emotions. When they get hungry, wet, or want to be held, they will cry to get what they need. The babies' only way to make sure they are heard is through the natural expression of crying (and crying and crying and...). As the babies grows into toddlers they continue to let you know their basic needs of hunger, love, and comfort. However, their list of needs usually expand by leaps and bounds with louder sounds and more behaviors to obtain the attention needed to satisfy those needs. As children get older their expanded list of needs starts sounding more like a list of demands to tell us over and over again what they expect. Similar to the baby's cry, children will instinctively express their feelings unless they are not allowed to do so by their caregivers.

Caregivers influenced your feelings

As a child, your laugh of joy, cries of pain and behaviors for attention were natural reactions to the experiences around you. If a caregiver responded to those reactions in a negative way, you would receive the message that your expressions were negative or bad. This is the time of life when caregivers were the most influential because of your dependence for all your needs. This was also the time when you were the most vulnerable because your caregiver's response and treatment to your needs shaped how you thought, felt, and behaved for the rest of your life. Your innocence was seen by the words and feelings you expressed. As a young child your self was made up of simple feelings and behaviors. You would say the first things that came out of your mouth and behave in whatever way first came into your mind. Consequently, whatever you said or did was an expression and extension of who you were and what you believed. How your caregivers responded to those expressions shaped your belief about yourself and determined how you would allow yourself to feel. You were dependent on your caregivers to learn how to identify and express feelings.

When eight-year-old Norma got hurt she went to her father with tears in her eyes and a pouting face. Her father said, "What are you crying about now? Go to your room and stay there until you stop acting like a baby." When Norma expressed pain, she reacted naturally with tears of sadness (God planned it that way!). The father's reaction gave Norma the message that her tears were wrong and she was sent to her room as if her behavior was unacceptable. Norma expressed a message through her tears, as if reaching out to say, "My tears are important," "I need to be comforted," "I need love." Because of her father's negative responses to her display of feelings, Norma developed the belief that experiencing sadness and expressing tears were wrong and unacceptable. Since her tears were an expression and extension of herself and who she was, Norma believed that she was wrong and unacceptable as well.

When caregivers repeat the same hurtful messages, the negative messages become stored in your mind. As a result, you will hear the same negative messages like a continuously playing tape recorder, "I cannot do anything right," "I'm not accepted," "I'm not good enough." These messages will form negative beliefs about yourself and begin the lifelong destructive pattern of self-judgment, self-doubt, and not-good-enough thoughts and feelings. When forty-year-old Dean came to my office he admitted that he became very embarrassed whenever he received a compliment from someone. When someone gave him a compliment, he would think, "I don't deserve it." When he finished a project at work he would say to himself, "I could have done better." He always had this underlying feeling he was never good enough. Dean described his mother as a perfectionist. Dean was expected to be a good boy but the expectations kept changing. No matter how hard he tried to please his parents, they would tell him to do more or they would not say anything at all. Dean realized he learned these negative feelings as a child and began to treat himself in the same negative way he was treated by his parents.

Not allowing you to feel

If you lived (or currently live) in a home where feelings are ridiculed or not allowed, it can become routine to stop thinking or saying what you're feeling. This is one way to escape the uncomfortable hurt you feel inside. Your mind has an amazing ability to shut out feelings as a way to survive shock or trauma that is too hard to bear. Unfortunately, many of these survival methods learned as a child, or adult, can become daily coping routines that are continued throughout life. Many of the survival methods including repressed memories, avoidance behaviors, feeling numb, and shutting off your emotions will be discussed later in the book.

During an appointment in my office, Fred described the fear he had of his alcoholic father. When Fred was a child his father regularly came home drunk, repeatedly yelling and making hurtful comments for reasons Fred never understood. Fred had nowhere to escape and had no alternative to the hurt his father would inflict. Fred learned very early that he had to stop feeling in order to survive. It was as if he would shut down emotionally so he would shut out the feeling of pain. Since shutting off his feelings was his learned reaction, Fred continued into adulthood this same method of not allowing himself to feel. As a result, whenever someone raised their voice, Fred would become afraid and automatically stop his emotions.

Suppressed feelings are harmful to your physical and emotional health

When emotions are buried under layers of hurts from the past, you are more prone to physical and emotional illness. The feelings that are pushed down (suppressed) will accumulate inside and fester like a disease that grows out of control. The suppression of feelings can create inner stress, which subsequently can hinder the production of brain chemicals that elevate your mood. Consequently, increase levels of stress can bring on feelings such as apathy, discouragement, anxiety, and depression. The accumulation of suppressed hurts and stress will build up pressure and show up through emotional illnesses within the mind or physical conditions in the body. For example, overwhelming anxiety and long-term feelings of unjust treatment can affect conditions of the stomach and digestion. Long-term unresolved grief, sadness, and hurt feelings can affect conditions of the lungs. Long-term unresolved issues of fear, dread, and shame can affect conditions of the kidney. Long-term anger and frustration can affect conditions of the liver.

What you do with your emotions has a direct impact on your physical and emotional well being. For example, headaches, ulcers, digestive problems, heart conditions, high blood pressure, Chronic Fatigue Syndrome, Fibromyalgia, eating and sleeping problems, impotence, anxiety, anger, depression, and a variety of other conditions of the mind and body are greatly influenced by the suppression of emotions. Researcher and professor Dr. Kenneth Pelletier wrote in his book Mind as Healer, Mind as Slayer (New York: Dell Publishing, 1977, p.117) that stressful experiences, especially in childhood, create within you certain methods of coping with your problems which become the routine for how you will handle stress later in life. Dr. Pelletier writes, "When this high stress level is prolonged and unabated [not changed], it produces alterations in neurophysiological functioning which can create the preconditions for the development of a disorder." In other words, when stress is held inside over time, your body and mind can begin to develop unhealthy thoughts and behaviors as methods to handle the inner turmoil. Holding in the stress from daily worries and conflicts creates a build up of pressure like a covered pot of water simmering on the stove. When the accumulation of tension and feelings build without the release of expressed feelings, the end result can be like a pot of boiling water bubbling over the rim. In time, the pot may erupt with an explosion if the steam is not released. The same is true for your physical reaction. You may be bubbling inside with reactions of stomach churning, body aches (especially head, neck, shoulders, and chest), shortness of breath, mood swings, irritability, anxiety, mental numbness, and a host of other symptoms. If you hold in feelings long enough, you may react like an explosion of steam through panic attacks, shaking, outbursts of words and emotion, physical violence, throwing objects, crying, and etc. For some, the explosion of steam may instead shut you down emotionally with reactions such as extreme apathy, a strong desire to get away, be alone, or desire to sleep. These feelings and behaviors can become so routine you have little understanding why you feel or act this way.

When Margo talked about her father during a counseling session, she became shaky and felt like her stomach was turning upside down. Although she could not remember many details of childhood memories, she remembered that her father was always yelling. While in counseling Margo realized she was afraid to be around her father. She always had a fear that something was going to happen. The only way for Margo to survive the emotionally traumatic experiences as a child was to not allow her self to feel. Although the fear was pushed deep inside, the childhood reactions of shaking, dread, and stomach churning continued into adulthood whenever someone was yelling.

Hurting emotions are all you know

Have you ever experienced a bad mood, irritability, anxiety, or felt uncomfortable around people and did not understand why you felt that way? Do you react with irritability, anxiety, moodiness, or anger on a regular basis? My counseling experience has shown that a major factor influencing how you react with another person is how you allow yourself to express feelings. (Medical problems, chemical imbalance, fatigue, and unresolved physical or emotional issues may also strongly influence these repeated emotional reactions.) When you have the same uncomfortable emotional responses with little understanding of why you feel that way, you find it easier to endure the hurt, rather than go through the pain of trying to change the uncomfortable emotional response. For example, stopping yourself from feeling hurt when someone yells at you is easier than trying to talk to the yelling person who is responsible for the hurt. Getting angry by raising your voice whenever someone questions your actions is easier than finding out that you may be wrong. Leaving the room whenever somebody starts to argue is easier than enduring the inner turmoil you feel. These emotional reactions can become so routine that they happen automatically and you assume there is nothing you can do about them.

When hurting emotions are all you know, you endure the same emotional reactions no matter how inconvenient, how uncomfortable, or how irrational the behaviors may be. You endure these emotional reactions because you may not know anything different or are afraid to open Pandora's box, stirring up pain you do not want to feel. Anxiety, anger, moodiness, fear, guilt, resentment, and other emotions were not intended to be part of your daily routine in such a way as to consume your life. God never intended people to be preoccupied with emotional or physical issues that take away from having a life of peace and joy. These emotional reactions become a source of turmoil and destruction that affects your mind, body, and soul, like an infection that does not heal. This infection can destroy your personal attitude, life outlook, spiritual well being, and deteriorate your physical and emotional health. Years of suppressed feelings leave a path of destruction that is masked with the belief that you deal with life without expressing your true feelings. When you lived in a home where you could not be truthful about your feelings, you will continue to live in a state of dishonesty with yourself. You will not be able to find true happiness. You will have difficulty getting your needs met because you will not be honest about your true feelings. You will have difficulty developing and/or maintaining close relationships because you never know what you feel inside. You will continue to struggle with inner emotional reactions such as hurts, anger, guilt, frustrations, and anxieties, as a part of the relationship. As a result, your relationships will suffer since you will struggle with how to identify and communicate emotions.

The importance of expressing your feelings

Your childhood is a training ground for learning how to handle stress, deal with people, and express feelings. There is a better chance of handling the problems of adulthood if you learn to handle life's ups and downs in your childhood. The better a person can handle stress, the happier the person will feel about life and the more successful their life will be as an adult. If you were not able to identify and express your hurts throughout the early years, it is less likely you will be able to successfully identify your feelings later in life. Drs. Fitzhugh Dodson and Ann Alexander, in their book, Your Child, Birth to Age 6 (New York: Simon & Schuster, 1986, p. 250), make the statement that it is very healthy for children to express positive and negative feelings. They write, "The inability to do so [express feelings], is one of the basic causes of many neurotic problems and psychosomatic diseases. The child who has learned not to express anger will be severely handicapped as an adult." For example, if you are not allowed to express feelings in healthy ways, the feelings will be expressed in unhealthy ways – either through emotional conditions such as anxiety and fears or through medical illnesses such as stress headaches and stomach aches. If you do not learn to express yourself in childhood, it will be more difficult to communicate your needs and your wants to others as an adult. Being able to freely and respectfully express yourself is how God planned for your mind and body to respond.

Even the Bible tells of people expressing anger, tears, fear, jealousy, sorrow, and joy. The wisdom of the Bible has been shown over thousands of years. It bears the truth that you were given feelings as a free gift from God as a vital part of your free will to express yourself. When you choose to use the many gifts given by God, you will be free from the hurts, anxiety, anger, unforgiveness, and oppression found through your daily experiences. You will find the inner freedom and peace of mind that are available through the release of feelings.

Feelings bring meaning to your life

Freely expressing your feelings allows you to explore inner emotions and bring meaning, purpose, and value to what is happening in your life. How many love songs, movies, or books have you seen, heard, or read about where lovers tell each other "I love you"? The feeling of love drives your desires and conveys an inner message of what you believe to be important. In the same way, saying statements that start with "I feel," or "I need," convey the meaning and importance to your inner needs and wants. Saying what you feel is an expression of what you believe is important. When someone hurts you, there is a violation against you as a person. The hurtful and disrespectful acts or comments are creating the belief that you are not important and you are not valued. If you have received hurtful words and acts over the years, you may believe that is normal. However, the hurtful treatment sends an underlying message that you are not good, worthless, not important, and undeserving. Hurtful treatment invades your heart, mind, and soul with disrespectful messages that you will repeat to yourself as an adult. This is seen in the disrespectful ways you treat yourself in thoughts or statements such as, "I'm not good enough to try that," or "I can't seem to do anything right," or "I might as well not say anything since I wouldn't say the right thing anyway." By using this type of thinking, you are mistreating yourself the same way you were mistreated years ago. This disrespect is a major reason why you cannot find meaning in your life. This treatment continues the destructive inner belief that you don't deserve to have a good life.

Feelings communicate what you believe and what you need. When you say statements such as "I feel hurt when you treat me that way," you are sending the message, "Stop treating me that way, I am important, and I do not like what you are doing to me." The statement identifies what is important to you and allows you to express your needs at the moment. Your ability to find purpose and a sense of joy in life has everything to do with freely identifying and expressing feelings. Statements such as, "I really feel good after walking each morning" bring purpose and value to what you are doing and give motivation to continue. However, if you struggle with feelings in your life, you will struggle with finding purpose and importance in life.

If you have held-in feelings you become a slave to the very hurts and pain you want to avoid. Each time you decide to hold in feelings and not express yourself, you are forging one more chain link to your bondage with misery. If you have been holding in feelings long enough, you may have frequent feelings of being overwhelmed or depressed, or experience a sense of numbness, void or emptiness inside. You may become overwhelmed easily, and want to avoid, escape, or hide from life situations. When you have a void in your life, you may experience what some people have described as being like a robot, going through the motions each day with little emotion, purpose, or direction. If this type of overwhelming, lifeless, purposeless experience sounds familiar, I've got great news. By learning to express your God-given feelings, you will break free from the overwhelming and lifeless existence that robs you of joy, peace of mind, purpose, and meaningful relationships.

Feelings are so important, God created them as part of your standard operating equipment. Feelings are not an option and you can freely use them without having to earn them or receive permission to express them. You have every right to express what was given to you and feel free to express your thoughts, needs, and desires. This book will help you learn more about yourself and teach you how to identify and express feelings in order to break free and live a life with the peace and joy God originally intended.

Chapter 2

How the past influenced your feelings

When I was a child, I used to speak as a child,
think as a child, reason as a child; when I became
a man, I did away with childish things.
(1 Corinthians 13:11)

When you were a young and innocent child the world was like a new kindergarten classroom full of exciting sights, sounds, and adventures. At that young age the experiences stirred up fear, tears, laughter, or whatever type of physical or emotional response the circumstances would trigger. God intended your responses to be an automatic natural reflex, like taking your next breath. God created you to react with laughter when something tickled your funny bone or to express tears when something hurt you. Each new experience became an emotional memory that was imprinted in your mind like a snapshot. How these early snapshots were collected and stored in the memory photo album of your mind greatly influenced how you handle life's ups and downs later in life. Let's learn how the early stages of development influenced your behavior and expression of feelings in order to begin making healthy changes.

How your caregivers influenced you

Raising children can be an honorable but scary responsibility for any caregiver. However, a common problem that caregivers talk about in counseling is the lack of training that comes with raising children. Whenever I meet with parents who have despair and guilt over the problems they believe they inflicted on their wayward child, I ask them "Which Parenting 101 class did you take before you had children?" There is no standard training in childcare. Unfortunately, child rearing is typically learned through on the job training. That leaves a lot of room for making mistakes and learning from those mistakes.

Like most men and women reading this book, your caregivers probably came from a childhood filled with hurt and pain. As a result they probably were dealing with their own hurts while raising you the best way they knew. Your caregivers responded toward you based on what they had learned from their caregivers. Even though patient, kind, unconditional love was what you longed for, your caregivers may not have always provided what you needed because they were not taught by the generation before them.

The primary caregivers in your childhood played an important role in shaping whether you felt safe and secure enough to openly express yourself while experiencing your expanding world. Your life was molded by the ability of the caregivers to meet your needs at each stage of development. You started out as a trusting child desiring love and attention from the significant people in your life. Consequently, this opened you up to whatever the caregivers brought your way, whether it was words of encouragement with loving arms or destructive words with hurtful hands. A caregiver's response to your physical and emotional needs was a critical influence in shaping what you believed, how you acted, and how you expressed yourself the rest of your life.

Infant years

As an infant you had a natural physical reaction of crying when something upsetting happened. You were too young to understand what was going on around you, so you simply reacted to the event. If you fell and bumped your head, pain was produced and the outcome of that physical hurt was a normal, emotional reaction of crying and wanting to be comforted. Your natural reaction to pain and fear is the most sophisticated system of cause and effect response designed by God. When you are hurt the nerve endings all over your body detect the point of hurt and register the pain in the brain. Your brain reacts with a response that is appropriate

24

at that stage of development. You can see this system working while caring for a newborn infant. The infant is very dependent on you for everything. They have an uncanny warning system, letting you know when they need food, burping, sleeping, holding, and changing! In fact, it almost seems as if they have a built-in radar system. They know exactly when to cry and holler – just at the moment you want to sit down, lie down, or talk on the phone! The crying is like a natural warning system for the infant to respond whenever there is physical discomfort. A response of warm hugs and comforting words will create an emotional foundation of safety and security to allow the infant to be free to express their feelings. Conversely, the lack of comforting responses will begin a shaky foundation of emotional insecurity.

Toddler years

As a toddler you spent most of your time exploring the environment and testing limits within that environment. If your parents reinforced limits and boundaries by telling you "no" whenever you got into something you shouldn't, an emotional confrontation may have taken place – which tested the caregiver's ability to reinforce those limits. When you did not want to hear "no," you would have natural expressions of anger, frustration, crying, and other outbursts of emotions when you rebelled against those boundaries. If the caregiver spanked you because you did not do what you were told, you experienced the natural sensation of physical pain, which should have produced an automatic, God-given response of crying. The crying was a natural reaction of expressing feelings and calling out for comfort.

Since experiencing bumps and bruises was so new, it was natural to occasionally look at your caregiver before you reacted, as if to help you determine how you should respond. If you fell down and lightly bumped your head, whether your caregivers immediately picked you up or yelled at you made a tremendous difference in your response. Regardless of how the caregiver responded, you were extremely vulnerable to the reactions of your caregivers. If the caregiver demonstrated consistent discipline with a caring touch, words of encouragement, setting limits and boundaries, chances are you experienced an emotionally and physically safe environment. This produced a sense of security and reinforced the notion that expressions of feelings were allowed and acceptable.

If the emotional responses of crying and laughing were not accepted, your world would not be physically safe, which reinforced the belief that expressing feelings was not accepted. When the caregiver would show inconsistent messages of acceptance and rejection, a sense of insecurity and uneasiness about what will happen next would be created. This insecurity would make you more apprehensive and less free to express yourself within your small world. During this stage of life you could not separate yourself as a person from the emotions that were produced. Consequently, if the caregivers became upset and yelled in the same room, whether it was about you or not, you may have automatically believed you were the reason for the yelling. You were too young to understand why there was yelling. All you knew was that it felt awful inside. If yelling and arguing of caregivers was frequently part of your young life, it probably created a sense of confusion, fear, anxiety, and a great apprehension to express yourself that carried into your later years. In addition, if the caregiver ridiculed your behaviors and emotional responses of laughter or crying, you would believe those behaviors and emotions were unacceptable.

Preschool and First School Years

During these years you had a simplified sense of right and wrong. Similar to the toddler stage, you did not have the reasoning ability to separate yourself as a person from accidents or bad behavior. When your caregiver yelled after you accidentally spilled milk, there was an automatic belief that spilling the milk was bad, with the additional belief "I must be bad" too. Since you could not understand the reason for something happening, you automatically assumed you were "bad" if a parent got angry – whether or not the anger was your fault. At this age, caregivers needed to be repeatedly clear as to why you were being punished. Living in a household with constant arguing and yelling could create a belief that you were bad, bad, bad. The worse you felt inside the stronger the belief was created that something was wrong. At this age you may not have understood the uncomfortable feelings inside, so your little mind only could rationalize with the belief there must be something wrong with you.

One of the ways to make sense in your small world was to internalize the feelings during a problem, believing it was your fault that the problem happened. This was also true for magical thinking, where you had difficulty separating fantasy from reality. If you wished for something that ac-

26

tually happened, you felt responsible for it happening. The feelings generated from situations such as death, separation, and divorce of a family member, or other traumatic events remained inside your mind for years to come. Several years ago a woman shared with me a childhood story that had haunted her all her life. When she was a child her mother said, "Breaking a mirror will bring bad luck." Soon after that comment was made, the unforgivable accident happened. One day when the little girl was playing with her make up kit, her little mirror broke when she dropped it on the floor. A few weeks later, her grandmother suddenly died. The little girl thought the only way to survive the guilt, hurt, and self-blame was to never admit her belief that she killed her grandmother. This incident helped to form the belief that holding in feelings was the best way to protect her self from feeling more pain.

This was an important time on the learning curve for the development of an inner belief of feeling loved and accepted by others. The amount of attention and approval received from caregivers played a large part in your belief of being loved and accepted. If your efforts to be Mommy or Daddy's little helper were met with frequent positive attention from the caregivers, chances are you developed a stronger sense of love and self-worth. If your help was often met with little attention and disappointment, you would often (as children do) shrug off the disappointment. However, after years of disappointments, it is hard to detect the hidden feelings of hurt, loss of love, and emptiness. In fact, you may rarely realize subtle issues later in your life like difficulty in getting close to someone for fear of being disappointed.

The primary people in your world continued to play an important role in allowing you to feel safe and secure enough to test the physical world no matter if you succeeded or failed. This process tested the patience and wisdom of your caregivers while allowing you to learn from your failures and express feelings. Learning to express your self with a continual diet of praise was needed for proper development. If you experienced frequent negative comments, the negativity either motivated you to try harder or increased your desire to give up. If the negativity became frequent enough, you shrugged it off by internalizing the failures that may have created a belief there was something wrong with you. The end result was a deep sense of insecurity about your self and your abilities. For example, if you fell down and skinned your knees, pain was produced. The outcome of that physical hurt should have been a normal emotional reaction of crying and a desire to seek a caregiver for comfort. If the caregiver did not provide the physical comfort of touch or emotional comfort of words, you should have felt hurt. If the lack of comfort was frequent, you would subtly create a deeper sense your feelings were not important. This often was translated to a belief that something was wrong with you.

During the period of fifteen months to about five years old, there was a need to strike a balance between independence, shame, and doubt. Caregivers who used compassionate words to teach right and wrong allowed you to succeed and fail with the encouragement to do better. This also allowed tantrums without the withdrawal of love that would encourage a healthy sense of shame. This shame was crucial and necessary as a balance for your newly discovered independence. It was the beginning of the reactions such as embarrassment, which was your normal human disappointments or shyness with strangers. However, when the caregivers' reactions were critical, demeaning, controlling, and ridiculing, there would grow an unhealthy sense of shame. You would not consciously understand the negative comments as unhealthy shame but as judgments against yourself that you would be at fault, undeserving or wrong.

School age years

During the school age years you continued to be sensitive to the hurtful words and actions of the adults and children in your life. You openly acted out feelings if the environment was safe enough to allow it to happen. You tended to deal with hurt, grief, and stress by internalizing the feelings with the outcome showing up through sadness, moodiness, eating problems, withdrawal symptoms, dreaming, and fantasies. For example, John described his home life with his alcoholic father as one big, blurred memory. His father sent him to his room often for reasons he never understood. Since there was little to do while lying in his room, he would go deep into a dream world. He would picture himself as a mighty hero able to fly away and rescue people in distress, especially little boys in distress who were trapped by monsters (like his father).

How the authority figures allowed you to express feelings in the home, school, and church continued to play a major part in sharing how you interpreted and expressed feelings the rest of your life. As you became older you may have begun to realize your emotional reactions were connected with events. If you lived in a no feelings, no talking about feelings home, you may not have learned the ability to connect feelings with events. During one counseling session, Joan described how she felt tense and very nervous whenever her boss became confrontational. Her reaction was so common she believed that was a normal response around authoritative people. In counseling, Joan remembered her experiencing fear and nervousness when her authoritative father confronted her. Her childhood reactions were so common it had become a way of life.

Trusting enough to express feelings

A sense of basic trust needs to be established in the early stages of your life. A belief needs to be imprinted that the world can be trusted and someone can be counted on to care for you. If you had a caregiver who was not predictable and did not respond to your physical and emotional needs of love and comfort, chances are you have more difficulty developing a sense of trust and a positive outlook toward life, and you have difficulty expressing your feelings. Without the development of security and trust, there may be more difficulty feeling safe enough to risk getting emotionally close to people and expressing your needs and/or inner feelings.

For most caregivers it is an ongoing balancing act to teach boundaries of appropriate behavior while creating a safe environment. Your ability to freely think, feel, and behave as an adult was greatly influenced by the sense of security that was created through the early interactions with your caregivers. The safety of your world and judgment of yourself was greatly influenced by your caregivers' response to your expressions. If the negative responses from caregivers became a way of life, the negativity was transformed into a very subtle sense of self-judgment that hung over you like a dark cloud. The other members of the family, friends, school, and church were also extremely important in building or destroying your perception and feelings about yourself. Caregivers who provided reassuring words and loving arms of comfort created a safe, trusting environment. That safe environment allowed you to feel safe enough to physically and emotionally express yourself. If the caregiver freely allowed you to approach them with physical hurts and expressions of emotions, a perception was created with the belief that your feelings were accepted and you were accepted. This built a sense of trust and security that gave you a freedom to express feelings. On the other hand, if you were not allowed to express your hurts and you were not comforted when you hurt, your little world did not seem safe enough to express much of anything. Your childhood mind would believe that your expressions were not accepted and you were not accepted. The lack of being accepted created a wedge between what you felt inside and your ability to express what you felt with others. This contributed to destructive thinking such as, I'm not important so my feelings do not matter.

Be careful not to blame

Now that you have learned how the past has influenced your feelings, your natural tendency is to wonder how and why your caregivers could let this happen. You may be angry, sad and hurt for the attention and protection you did not receive. You may be angry and blame yourself for allowing others to take advantage of you. You may be like people I see in my office who become angry at themselves for allowing their uncle, grandparents, parents, or others to hurt them. "I should have known better," some would say. You cannot blame yourself for what you did not know. As a child, your natural desire was to trust others until you learned otherwise. Your job was to be the child. The job of the significant adults in your life was to be a caregiver. You were supposed to be protected and provided love and comfort by the adult, which is why they were called caregivers. You cannot be responsible for the poor judgment and poor choices of your caretakers or other people who hurt you.

Blaming God

You may blame God for what you believe He allowed to happen. You may be angry and resentful that God did not answer your prayers throughout the years. As a result, you may not want to have anything to do with God, or you may not have felt very close to Him over the past years. You may believe that God is very powerful and should have saved you from your hurts. The truth is, God is very powerful, but He was not the one who hurt you. You live in a world full of sin and hurtful people. The hurts came from the choices of the people in your life. God created everyone with the freedom to make choices, good or bad, and prefers people to make good choices. Unfortunately, you may have been hurt by the bad choices people made. Most importantly, God does not want you to be hurt and no matter what you have heard or felt over the years, it was not God's or your fault that someone else made the bad choice to hurt you.

You are allowed to be disappointed and angry about what happened to you. However, you must realize that God loves you more than anything in this world. In fact, God so loved the world that He gave His one and only Son that whoever believes in Him shall not perish but have eternal life (see John 3:16). This also refers to you. God gave His only Son, Jesus Christ, so you may live with the love and peace He wants to give to you. Even if you were the only person on this earth God still would have given His one and only Son for you. In your time of hurting, God was hurting too. As your Heavenly Father, He understood then and understands now what you must go through in this hurtful world. He wants you to find comfort from Him to find the strength to overcome your hurts. "The LORD is close to the brokenhearted and saves those who are crushed in spirit' (Psalm 34:18).

You may say, "I never felt God's presence. He never answered my prayers." When you were hurting inside, you probably had a hard time trusting anyone (including God). If you had difficulty identifying feelings, the roller coaster of negative emotions stirring inside would also make it difficult to feel the presence of God. As a general rule, you cannot trust your negative feelings when you want to find God. Feelings will fool you and Satan will use hurtful feelings as a weapon against you. You must trust in the Holy Word of God. The Bible is full of promises that you can use for strength. "...God has said, Never will I leave you; never will I forsake you. So we say with confidence, 'The Lord is my helper; I will not be afraid. What can man do to me?" (Hebrews. 13:5,6).

Blaming your caregivers

You may blame your caregivers for what has happened. As mentioned earlier in this chapter, your caregivers most likely came from hurtful pasts themselves. That does not justify or sanction their hurting you, but it may provide some understanding of why it happened. Your caregivers learned from the generation before them how to respond (or not to respond) to you. The good traits and the bad traits will be handed down to the next generation. In the Bible you read, "You [God] show love to thousands but bring the punishment for the fathers' sins into the laps of their children after them..." (Jeremiah 32:18). In other words, the sins of former generations will be passed on to the children of the next generation. God did not like it when your caregivers allowed their job, money, alcohol, control, authority, neglect, or temper to keep them from loving you. God does not want these hurts to be passed on to you or the next generation. By reading this book you are taking the first steps toward stopping the destructive generational patterns. Your caregivers learned from the treatment and information they obtained from their caregivers. Do not let the destructive thoughts of blame turn into resentment, anger, and hate. These thoughts will destroy you with unhealthy emotional and physical problems that will take away your ability to receive peace and joy in your life.

Be encouraged, there is hope! You have the power to stop the unhealthy patterns from destroying you and from infecting the next generation! As you learn more about the destructive patterns of hurt and shame, pray that you can make a decision, right now, to stop those patterns. As you continue reading this book, pray for the ability to see the destructive patterns from the generations before you. And pray for the wisdom of how to stop those patterns, in order to prevent the destruction in the future. You have a unique opportunity to stop the destructive cycle of hurt and unhealthy patterns with you and your generation. The good news is that if you choose to make healthy changes in your life, no other generation has to be subjected to the same cycle of hurts and unhealthy patterns that you received.

The early influences of your home life and caregivers were a major part in the development of the emotional, physical, and spiritual growth of your life. As a child you were helpless to the people and environment around you. The emotional responses and physical behaviors learned during your childhood will remain the same for the rest of your life unless you make the decision to change. How the past hurts and painful memories affected your life will be discussed in the next chapter.

PS: Words of encouragement

Now that you have read this chapter, there are probably many thoughts about your past flooding through your mind. You may be asking, "Why did my past happen this way?" You may need to be comforted right now from the hurts you have stirring inside. These hurts may be feelings of sadness, anger, bitterness, or unforgiveness toward your caregivers, yourself, or God. Take heart! Lift your head up high! You are in a healthy process of discovering about yourself and learning what needs to change for a healthy future. Think of yourself standing at a gate looking down the pathway of emotional healing. You are beginning to walk through that gate down that path toward the goal of a healthy mind, heart, and soul. If you need to do something with what you are feeling, give yourself permission to tell someone what you think or feel. You can:

1. Pray.
2. Write your thoughts down.
3. Talk to someone.

Chapter 3

Protecting yourself from your hurts

So do not fear, for I am with you; do not be
dismayed, for I am your God. I will strengthen you and help you;
I will uphold you with my righteous right hand.
(Isaiah 41:10)

Like many of the men and women I see in my office, you may have grown up (or are now living) in a home that is like a war zone with battles raging all around. You may have lived in a war of conflict with a constant barrage of yelling, hitting, and threats like bomb explosions that cause physical hurts and pain. You may have lived in a home with a subtle war of mind games with constantly changing or unreachable expectations and rigid rules. You may have lived in a home with constant ridicule, insults, and negative comments that destroy a person from the inside out, like chemical warfare. Or a home where the spouse or caregivers provided basic physical needs such as food, shelter, and occasional outings, but were unavailable to meet your emotional needs of loving expressions of hugs and kisses, verbal reassurance, and trust.

The battle wounds of pain and suffering from a daily dose of emotional or physical explosions, mind games, and negative comments were stuffed deep inside for survival. Over the years, it may have begun to be more difficult to suppress the hurts like an overstuffed suitcase you couldn't close. Once you stuff too many pieces of clothing in the suitcase, you must do something to push it closed. The same is true for stuffing feelings. The more hurts and pain you stuff inside, the more you will need something to protect yourself from feeling that pain. You will create behaviors to avoid situations in your life that may trigger hurtful feelings. There are many creative ways you learned to protect yourself from becoming hurt or allowing yourself to feel. These protective behaviors may have become so common that you do not see beyond those behaviors, even if the behaviors do not make sense. It is time to free yourself from the destructive behaviors that hold you hostage and do not allow you to freely express your feelings.

Avoiding emotional hurts as a child

As you read in the previous chapter, much of your emotional growth during the early stages of development was greatly influenced by role modeling and acceptance of emotions from your caregivers. Healthy interactions and acceptance of feelings promoted healthy emotional growth that would allow the expression of feelings to mature into the next stage of development. You also read in the previous chapters that your mind has a powerful way of shutting down or suppressing hurts that are too painful to experience. As a natural protection from the repeated hurts and traumas that came from unhealthy interactions, your mind stopped allowing you to feel at the point of the trauma. During these hurtful experiences you shut down (become stuck) emotionally as if your emotions were suspended in time. Becoming emotionally stuck literally stopped your emotional development. Your mind stopped the painful feelings as a protection against the hurt over which you had little control. As a result, you would create behaviors to avoid the hurt. These behaviors would become your normal response to similar hurtful experiences in your life.

What if your caregivers had a bad day and you got caught in the crossfire of yelling, hitting, or whatever emotional explosion was thrown your way? It was easy to become overwhelmed with feelings of hurt, fear, confusion, anxiety, sadness, and a host of other emotions. You experienced the caregivers' emotional explosions like machine gun-fire with little ability to sort out the different feelings whirling inside. It may have been difficult to analyze why or what you were specifically feeling. Your mind and body might have automatically reacted as if you were trying to get away from a hive of attacking bees. If the yelling and emotional explosions were the typical daily scenarios at home, you developed routine ways to survive each little traumatic episode to shield yourself from the sensations that were too painful to feel. As you grew older, you used the learned survival techniques or avoidance behaviors to shield yourself from the hurt when people confronted you with nasty words, yelling, arguments, hitting, or other confrontations. This chapter will describe the survival techniques that have become a way of life to protect your self from feelings that would surface during hurtful experiences.

Avoidance behaviors

When hurtful situations happened as a child, you may have adjusted by taking on behaviors to avoid the feelings of hurt, pain, or fear. Avoidance behaviors can come as a result of the hurtful comments and actions of others or from events such as divorce, death, or absence of a loved one. You may have avoided the hurts by keeping yourself physically busy, like cleaning your room, watching television, or playing with friends. You may have daydreamed, played in a fantasy world, or rationalized yourself through the experience. It became easier and less threatening to ignore and push down the feelings, rather than to allow yourself to feel the pain. If the hurts were overwhelming, you may have survived by separating the emotional pain from your physical being. This is where your mind literally shut off in order to mentally handle the amount of hurtful stimulus coming in at one time. You often learned to adapt by automatically shutting down your sense of emotion, as if in a state of numbness, or mental block. This made it easier to continue living a "normal" life while living in an abnormal, hurtful world. How you were conditioned to deal with feelings in your early years can often transfer into adulthood. Avoidance behaviors may become so common, you consider them as a normal part of your life, no matter how unhealthy or destructive they had become.

As a child, Joan spent most of her time in her bedroom. She described many occasions when she was sent to her room for punishment. However, most of her memories were playing in her room to avoid the fighting and arguing that went on between her parents. Joan developed a creative fantasy world to spend hours and hours with imaginary playmates. Joan found a safe haven in her room where she could hide from the hurts of her world.

Numbing and blocking feelings

The numbing effect is where your mind emotionally shuts down to protect yourself from further hurts and disappointments that you feel inside. That was the point when your mind did not register the pain, like your mouth going numb when the dentist gave you a shot of painkiller. Your mind may block out feelings, like turning to a television channel that was fuzzy white from poor reception. This process became standard operating procedure to protect your self from painful experiences that were too hard to bear or from years of hurts. This is especially true when growing up in homes where you were not allowed to feel or talk about your feelings. As a result, you may be aware of your pain or discomfort, but you did not learn to identify those sensations and connect them with the hurtful event. Instead you would automatically feel the discomfort and then push away the pain. After years of practice, shutting out feelings became as routine as blinking your eyes. When you are asked about your feelings you may say, "I don't feel anything" or "My mind goes blank." Or, you may experience confusion or have little emotional reaction after a hurtful event.

During a counseling session Ruth described the fear that came from her husband's controlling and threatening behavior. She later realized she never allowed herself to express feelings as a child in fear that something worse would happen. When Ruth began to cry, I asked her to tell me how she felt at the moment. There was a long pause before she said, "I don't know. It's hard for me to find the words." Ruth realized she continued into adulthood the difficulty of allowing herself to identify and express feelings, just as she did as a child living with her controlling father.

Repressing memories

Hurtful feelings and memories may be pushed deep inside (repressed) for years with little reoccurrence of clear memories. Many times painful memories can be repressed when a traumatic event happened, as a way for your mind to protect you from the pain. That is frequently a point in time where the emotional development became stuck. Often events that happen later in life can trigger feelings, flashbacks, nightmares, depression, or other medical or emotional symptoms. It is very important that you be allowed to unravel these painful repressed memories at your own pace. Repressing the memories becomes most evident with people I see who cannot remember a block of time in their childhood. For many adults these were periods of time that are blank, like looking at a blank television screen. I am not referring to memories you consciously don't want to remember, like the times you visited old aunt Mabel who made you eat cauliflower and always gave you a big wet kiss. I am referring to those blocks of time that were absent from your memory which consisted of a number of years or a major part (or all) of your childhood. No one (not even a therapist) should expect a person to move faster than you are emotionally ready. The hurtful experiences that you have remembered may not be as traumatic as those found in repressed memories.

A man I had been seeing in my office had mentioned the fear of dark, enclosed places. When going to bed at night he typically had to leave a light on with the door open to the bedroom. If he would wake up with the lights off, the darkness would cause heightened anxiety, shortness of breath, fear, and subsequent panic attacks. In counseling, he recalled a childhood memory where he was often shut in a confined dark space by a baby-sitter as a form of punishment. To emotionally survive as a child, he shut down his feelings during the overwhelming situation. The subsequent feelings of helplessness, fear, panic, vulnerability, anger, and mistrust of the baby-sitter were not expressed at the time because of fear that something bad might happen. Consequently, he repressed the trauma of being scared in the dark. Since he did not have the opportunity to deal with the feelings at the time, the traumatic event was repressed, with the feelings continuing to fester inside for years to come. Later in his adult life, situations such as a darkened room would trigger the overwhelming fear originally produced many years earlier.

Rationalizing feelings

Another way for you to survive the pain would be to rationalize away the disappointment by making an excuse for yourself or others. As the disappointment or hurt continued, rationalization was the best way at the moment to survive the hurt and a way to find some understanding of the other person's hurtful behavior. On most days young Joe would come home from school wishing his father would play ball with him only to be disappointed to find his father lying on the couch sleeping or watching television. "I'm too tired after working. Leave me alone." his father would repeatedly say. Joe's mother would reinforce his father's response by saying, "Can't you see your father is tired after working all day?" Joe would rationalize the repeated feelings of rejection by feeling sorry for his father. Joe would never allow himself to acknowledge his feelings of rejection and hurt. As these situations continued over the years, it became more common for Joe to rationalize other circumstances as a way to deal with his feelings. As Joe became older, rationalization became a way of life. Joe continued to make excuses for other people whenever they would disappoint or hurt him. He realized this made it difficult for him to adequately express his inner feelings and get his emotional needs met.

Childlike reactions as an adult

When you created avoidance behaviors to protect yourself from the childhood hurts, you may have slowed your emotional growth or became emotionally stuck at that age. As a result, you physically matured into an adult body but your emotions did not grow up with you. It was as if your emotions stopped maturing, or became stuck at the age of the hurt. You learned to adapt so well to your childlike feelings, you didn't even realize you were emotionally stuck. You would often see the childlike behavior in others first, before you would recognize it in yourself. As an adult, you may have experienced this when your emotional reactions to a hurtful situation did not seem to fit the way you physically behaved. One person described this experience as being like having the little child in them feeling hurt while the physical adult body continued on with life. Donna was at the age of seven when she remembered routinely running to her room and jumping under her covers whenever her father was hurtful. Going to sleep was the only way she had learned to make herself avoid the hurt. Donna described her current behavior of going to bed and sleeping as a way of avoiding the hurt she experienced from the arguments with her husband. As a way to escape her feelings, Donna continued into adulthood the same behaviors she had learned as a child.

Becoming emotionally stuck can also be seen when you act out behaviors that do not fit your adult age. When you became frustrated, disappointed, or angry you may have acted out your emotion in a childlike reaction. When demands or circumstances were beyond your emotional comfort level, you reacted in a manner that reflected the age at which you had become emotionally stuck. This is when your thoughts, feelings, and behaviors resemble a child's level of response rather than an adult response. Reacting with childlike reactions while you are an adult does not make you immature, wrong, or a bad person. You are simply continuing patterns of responses you learned to use as a way to survive as a child. You often do not recognize the childlike behaviors since they are masked by the way you talk and act as an adult. When Sam became frustrated during arguments with his wife he would use put-down statements toward his wife as if to get in the last word. He would stomp his feet as he left the room and slam doors on his way out of the house. Sam would easily become defensive and not talk to his wife for several days after an argument. When his wife talked to Sam's mother it was discovered that he would often get his way as a child and temper tantrums were a frequent occurrence. Finally his wife's eyes were open to seeing Sam's behavior as a childlike temper tantrum in an adult body.

As an adult you physically interact with other adults but you emotionally react to situations with a childlike emotional sense of feeling and response. This emotional reaction becomes so routine for you that people rarely can identify this as a problem. It is important that people do not become discouraged when discovering they are using childlike reactions in adulthood. I must emphasize again that you are not immature, wrong, or a bad person if you discover childlike reactions. On the contrary, you are making important discoveries to begin the necessary changes to a healthy, adult, emotional response. Once you recognize this childlike reaction and take responsibility for your actions, you are in store for great healing to take place. Childlike reactions are described in more detail in Chapter Nine, Discovering and overcoming how your past influenced you.

When the going gets tough, you get going

When there are tempers flaring, arguments, yelling, or general conflict, do you leave the room or have an urge to get away? Does your head ache, stomach churn, heart race? Do you become nervous, uncomfortable, have an urge to hide, or want to go to bed and stay there? When you feel threatened or unsafe does your mind kick into the fight or flight mode? This is where your mind signals the production of adrenaline to assist the body to either fight back or high tail it out of there. Your mind and body react to survive as a child and you will continue the same patterns of survival as an adult unless you learned different response patterns. You may feel it is easier to handle the situation by getting away rather than staying and feeling like you will fall apart. Your first clue may be the upset stomach or chest pressure you get when there is conflict around you. Many describe a feeling of dread or fear that something will happen.

Ted described himself as a self-directed, hard-working person. However, he never understood why his stomach became very nervous, with a desire to get away when someone made a negative comment about his work. During counseling, Ted remembered the childhood feeling of not being good enough when his parents would criticize him. He forgot about the childhood nervousness he experienced. Ted finally realized the feelings buried deep inside were carried into adulthood.

Keeping people at a distance

Do you have a hard time making or keeping friends? Do you feel like running whenever someone gets emotionally close? Is it difficult to trust others? Past hurts have a way of not allowing you to be loved and make it hard to freely express love with others. To protect your- self, you stop inner feelings and keep the other person at a distance in order not to be hurt. I had been meeting with a woman who admitted she did not feel love from her husband and found it hard to say, "I love you." The woman acknowledged she had a good marriage and a husband who freely showed his love toward her. She grew up in a stable home with her parents. They did not express their feelings and showed minimal affection toward one another. While growing up, the woman was emotionally distant from her mother but had a close relationship with her father. In the woman's late teen years, her father suddenly died without her saying goodbye. She described other close male relationships that left emotional scars from hurtful experiences. In retrospect, the woman realized she had allowed herself to become emotionally close in past relationships that ended with devastating results. She never learned how to identify her feelings of hurt and sadness that came from the hurtful past. As a result, the pain was held tightly inside like a box with an airtight lid. She decided not to open the lid for fear her inner feelings would become vulnerable to more hurts. Each time a relationship became emotionally close, she would shut down emotionally and stop her feelings, without knowing why. The hurtful relationships in her life made a great impact on her inability to trust and allow others to get emotionally close. She later learned to identify the inner feelings and felt safe enough to express her hurt and sadness to her husband. This allowed the woman to resolve many of the past hurts and begin to allow room in her heart for the love she longed for.

Have you ever been with a person who rarely said anything, consistently changed the subject, or constantly told you what was on their mind and would not stop to let you get a word in? In many cases, what these people have in common is difficulty letting anyone get emotionally close or letting others into their life. Their quietness or incessant talking can be like a shield to either protect from getting hurt or from expressing their true feelings. As odd as it may sound, it is easier to not be loved, not say anything, or say too much than allow someone to truly know you. Unfortunately, you rarely are aware this is happening. The only way to help this type of person is to gently speak to them about how it makes you feel when they behave this way. You may need to do a lot of explaining to help them understand just what they are doing that creates the feeling in you. Chances are they grew up in a no feeling, no talk about feelings family where feelings were not allowed to be discussed. Behaviors were created for protection against getting hurt after becoming too emotionally close.

Food and eating issues

Eating can be a physical form of comfort and protection from emotions that hurt. Food can often be used as a substitute to deal with feelings associated with issues such as hurt, fear, failure, conflict, losing control, loneliness, or fear that something bad will happen. Food is one of the most powerful substances that can subtly influence your life to the point of life or death. Some find comfort from eating where others can find disgust. And still others can have both sensations battling inside.

Susan described herself as a chocoholic. Whenever she became upset or depressed she would have a craving to eat chocolate. She would only find momentary comfort in this habit. Depending on the amount of chocolate, the next day she might experience sadness, lack of motivation, headaches, or irritability, and feel physically worse than before she ate the chocolate. Often she would feel emotionally depressed and hate herself for eating unhealthy foods. However, the cycle would happen all over again if she became upset. Susan found out that foods such as chocolate can change your brain chemistry and raise your the blood sugar, giving you a momentary and artificial mood elevation. The higher the blood sugar (which made her feel good), the lower the blood sugar would fall hours later (which made her feel depressed). This severe blood sugar cycle created more depression and severe mood swings. The emotional roller coaster within Susan was physically unhealthy and destroyed her ability to detect true feelings.

Since food is so readily available and a life-sustaining substance, it is a major power in your life. How food was provided and available in your childhood years can influence what you do with it the rest of your life. Unknowingly you connect memories, behaviors, and feelings around food. Food may be a form of protection from a loss, a point in time you were ridiculed, or protection from not feeling good about yourself. Janet described her mother as a very busy woman, not having much time for her. When Janet asked her mother to play with her or she wanted comfort, Janet often received a cookie or something sweet. It was no surprise that as an adult, Janet frequently found comfort from sadness, loneliness, or upset feelings by eating sweets. Sweets became a substitute for love, comfort, and attention. They were easier and quicker to reach when she was lonely or hurt and she did not have to worry about being rejected.

In your mind you know you should not overeat, especially when you look down at the bathroom scale. But for some reason you cannot help the urge to stuff your face. Some of you may feel like you're driven by a mysterious power or inner monster that takes over your will – as if the monster will not allow you to be in control of your own feelings, actions, and life! There is a confusion between logic and emotion, as though a battle is going on inside. When damaged emotions are involved, you tend to be motivated to eat because of emotional reasons and the logic gets thrown out the window. It is as if you lost control over your life and what you put into your mouth is the last part of your life over which you have any control. Others tell you what to do, where to go, how to feel (usually how not to feel), and who you are supposed to be. Somehow you believe food gives you power and control over your life. Unfortunately, it never seems to work that way because food becomes like the sneaky devil that prowls around fooling and deceiving you. You may begin to believe you have more control because you can decide what and when to put food in your mouth. The food gives a false sense of being in control — which only satisfies you for a short time. Since you believe you cannot change your situation, you develop a sense of helplessness. Because you never learned how to express your feelings, they become trapped inside, which increases your sense of being out of control, like a little child helplessly sitting on a tricycle that is racing down a hill. Food becomes your expression of control, similar to placing your feet on the ground to control the fast moving tricycle. As soon as you pull up your feet the tricycle becomes out of control again. As a little child you needed someone trustworthy to teach you the dangers of riding a tricycle down hill. The same is true for you as an adult. In order to stop your life from feeling like it is racing out of control, you need to trust the help that others can give. Allow yourself to receive the help you may need.

Addictive behavior

There are more types of addictive behaviors and reasons for the addictions than I have room for in this book. However, among the deeper reasons for many additive behaviors is the inability to deal with life's hurts and feelings. For example, substances such as alcohol, some prescription medications, and street drugs often cloud the mind in order to quickly get away from what you cannot handle. Have you heard someone say that they drink to help relax, feel more socially acceptable, get away from it all, or talk more easily? Drugs and alcohol are simply mind-altering substances that decrease inhibitions and allow you to be something you normally cannot be without them. Those statements expose the fact that there is more going on inside than you can handle. Rarely will you find a regular substance user who can openly deal with daily conflicts, arguments, and feelings in a healthy way. Whether it is drugs, alcohol, pornography, gambling, food, or any other addition, if you need the habit to make you feel good or forget about your problems, you have lost control of your life. The habits you use to help you get through life have clouded your ability to know the truth about your inner feelings.

You were made in the image of God and your body is considered a Temple. "Don't you know that you yourselves are God's temple and that God's spirit lives in you? If anyone destroys God's temple, God will destroy him; for God's temple is sacred, and you are that temple." (1 Corinthians 3:16-17) When you are involved with habits that are negatively affecting your body, you are destroying the Temple that God entrusted you to use while on this earth. By caring for the Temple God gave you, you are honoring God and yourself.

Although the healing process for addictive behaviors is very complex, there is an extreme need to find new ways to release your past hurts and daily frustrations. You cannot take away the habit that is being used to deal with life's problems without replacing it with something else which must be just as helpful or gratifying. First, you must want help for yourself and then there must be some meaningful reason for you to change. I have discovered the general rule that people will not change unless there is something important they will lose if they do not change. Does your habit mean so much that you will not change unless your own life (and those around you) depends on it? You do not need to destroy yourself with an unhealthy habit that will only create more destruction and misery in your life. It is never too late to make a change. It often takes someone or something to help you see that you are a slave to the destructive habit.

Protecting your self from hurts started out as a natural reaction in childhood for survival during the battles in your little world. You would not know how to react any differently unless you were taught other behaviors to take their place. Your natural tendency would be to carry the protective behaviors into adulthood by adapting the childlike protective reactions or behaviors into your adult situations. It is easier to look at another person and say, "They are acting so childish," than it is to see it within your self. This is especially true if you used the same avoidance behaviors or protective reactions all your life. The good news is you have now become aware of these behaviors and you can do something positive to change them. In the next chapter you will learn about the bondage of shame that led you to creating protective behaviors. This will help you become victorious in making healthy changes.

PS: Words of encouragement

All of this information may be overwhelming right now. It may be like an immovable mountain in front of you or a big weight on your shoulders. You may feel like there is too much wrong with yourself to even try to change. Be encouraged, there is hope! Just be patient and gentle with yourself at this important time in your healing process. Let's take one step at a time to help you make healthy changes. Jesus tells you, "Come to Me, all you who are weary and burdened, and I will give you rest. Take My yoke upon you, and learn from Me, for I am gentle and humble in heart; and you will find rest for your souls" (Matthew. 11:28-29). With God's help and continued reading, you will begin to feel the changes. If you need to do something with what you are feeling, continue to:

1. Pray to God.
2. Write your thoughts down.
3. Talk to someone.

Chapter 4

When you are shamed

Why are you downcast, O my soul? Why so disturbed
within me? Put your hope in God, for I will yet
praise Him, my Savior and my God.
(Psalm. 43:5)

Do you ever feel that you must work twice as hard to get acceptance or that you cannot seem to quite measure up to what is expected, no matter how hard you try? Do you ever believe you are different than others, unable to be good enough, undeserving, unwanted, unworthy, weak, unlovable, ashamed, and you can't seem to change it? Do you feel like your opinion, thoughts, and feelings do not count? Is it hard to tell others how you really feel? This is the product of a shame nature identity and the self-judgment that shame brings into your mind, heart, and soul. Shame nature identity is a side effect of unhealthy relationships where hurtful emotional, physical, and spiritual messages are commonplace. The hurtful words and actions that criticize, insult, and ridicule give you the message your identity is flawed, deflective, undeserving, and not good enough; it is as if something is inherently wrong with you.

During a counseling session, Joann had tears well up in her eyes as she said, "I'm such a failure. I can't do anything right." When I asked her what it was that made her a failure, she covered her face with her hands and burst into tears. "Nothing I do is ever good enough for my husband or my kids. I'm such a failure! I'm such a failure!" After years of ridicule from the husband, Joann finally let out her inner most beliefs about herself.

The underlying destructive message that you are somehow not able to measure up has penetrated your inner beliefs, emotions, and behaviors. This is most evident in your belief that you do not have a right to express your thoughts or feelings. You may believe the opinions of other people are worthy, but you believe what you think and feel are unworthy and undeserving. You may be uneasy about giving your opinion or lend a hand believing you may not do a good job. As a result, you do not let others know what you think or feel. You don't want to embarrass yourself around others because you believe what you say or do is inferior or insignificant. When someone says unkind words, your shame nature identity makes you believe the statements are true. When someone behaves unkindly, your shame makes you believe you deserve that behavior. Shame is among the most powerful stumbling blocks to allowing you to express inner feelings. The shame nature identity is carried through your life, distorting beliefs, crippling relationships, and continuing the destruction of self-judgment. You become enslaved to the destructive thoughts and actions of shame. You are crippled with the belief you somehow deserve the hurt and misery that comes with feeling you are not good enough to deserve better.

Healthy shame

You must understand that healthy shame is a normal human emotion shaped by healthy relationships in your early life. Healthy shame gives you a sense of identity through boundaries and humility that can help define your moral sense of right and wrong. Shame is the knowledge of being wonderfully different from others. "For my thoughts are not your thoughts neither are your ways my ways, declares the Lord" (Isaiah. 55:8). As a child, shame brings healthy respect of authority, believing that consequences will happen if you do something wrong. You need shame as a balance to keep yourself on a morally correct path. Healthy shame gives you the belief you did something wrong when the ball you threw went flying the neighbors' window. When you walk off the morally right path, your healthy shame should be strong enough to make you think something is wrong enough to motivate you back toward the right path.

Origins of unhealthy shame

The essence of unhealthy shame can be experienced in the general forms of unhealthy physical, verbal, and nonverbal messages that come from relationships throughout your life. The words and actions received from parents, friends, teachers, extended family, and the church during the childhood years tend to be the most common to produce unhealthy shame. As a child, you started out like a new block of soft white clay. Your young mind was fresh and clean and naturally trusted what people said or did with you. The fresh clay made you very vulnerable to the shame that came from the unhealthy messages. Each time someone gave a hurtful message, it was like a spot of dirt that stuck to the clay. After repeated unhealthy physical, verbal, and nonverbal messages, the clay became dirtier and dirtier. The dirty spots appeared so subtly that you didn't even notice a change. As the clay filled with dirt, the dark pieces of filth made the clay harder. Little by little the clay changed color and became hard and brittle. The condition of the clay changed in ways you didn't even notice.

The changing of the clay is similar to how shame came into your life. With one little comment or action you didn't believe any harm could be done. Each hurtful message was a dirt spot that spread over the clay like cancer taking over your body. You were so accustomed to the dirt you didn't realize the cloud over your soul that brought darkness to your life. If the hurtful messages continued over the years, you did not recognize the hardening of your heart that made it more difficult to allow love, joy, and peace of mind in your life. All you knew was that inside you always felt dirty, undeserving, unlovable, and unworthy. You believed that what you said and thought was not good enough – so why say anything?

Like a fresh block of clay, you innocently started out with the trust that what you were told was the truth. If you received unhealthy messages, your heart, mind, and soul were hurt like the stabbing of a small knife. The hurt began to act like as a barrier, blocking your heart and mind from expressing inner thoughts and feelings. The hurts were pushed deep inside, creating the belief you were too unworthy to let them out. Holding in your feelings became the root of a multitude of life problems such as, poor communications, unhealthy relationships, destructive thoughts and feelings, unhealthy behaviors, and emotional/medical conditions.

Unhealthy shame can happen at any age with any relationship where there is a basic lack of respect that is harmful toward the other person. As an adult, you are susceptible to the hurts of shaming from a spouse, ex-spouses, family, employers, friends, coworkers, and the church. If unhealthy shame was a part of your childhood, you may not easily detect shaming messages as an adult. If unhealthy messages became a routine in your adult relationships, you would experience the same spreading of shame in your heart, mind, and soul. As shame became a part of your life you developed unhealthy responses as a way to deal with the feelings of shame. For example, let's say you just got a call from your mother saying she was going to "drop off" something for you. You rush around the house like a mad hornet, trying to clean from top to bottom, as if you were guilty of something before anything was proven wrong. You work hard, trying to make everything good enough for people as if you need to prove yourself. You typically find it difficult to feel good about what you do or say.

The origin of unhealthy shame can be so subtle that you do not notice how it affects your life. This is especially true when shame started as a common part of your early years. Let's explore some of the possible origins for the shame nature in order to help you identify unhealthy shame and begin the healing to your heart, mind, and soul.

Verbal shaming

The verbal comments that come from others can mortally cut you with deep, lasting wounds. Children are especially wounded by hurting words that come from adults and other children. Even the Bible reflects, "All kinds of animals, birds, reptiles and creatures of the sea are being tamed and have been tamed by man, but no man can tame the tongue. It is a restless evil, full of deadly poison" (James 3:7-8). Since you often say what is important in your life, your thoughts, ideas, and opinions communicate your needs, desires, and wants. As a child, if you went to your caregiver with tears of hurt rolling down your cheeks, you were communicating how you felt inside. You were communicating through your actions, I want to be comforted from my pain. If the caregiver responded, "What's wrong with you now?" or "Go away can't you see I'm busy?" or "Stop your crying!" you were given the message your tears were not acceptable. If this happened often enough, you would begin to believe you were not important because your hurts were not important.

Verbal forms of shame can become so common that you don't know you are being shamed. Whether you realize it or not, what is said to you can be even more damaging than physical hurts. During a counseling session, a man said he wished his father had physically beat him rather than use hurtful words. "At least the beatings would have healed," he said. The ridicule, name calling, and verbal put downs all have a deep wounding affect. Phrases like "You dummy, why did you do it that way?" "You're so stupid," or "You're an idiot," are all shame messages that make you believe you are defective, wrong, unhealthy, and not good enough.

Blame and guilt

Many times an underlying sense of fault, blame, and guilt come with the statements we hear, such as "Look what you've done now!" or "Because of you, I can't..." or "Now look what you've done!" When you lived in a family that had poor relationships, parental separation, divorce, or marital strife you were (or still are) often caught in the middle of negative energy and hurtful comments that bounced back and forth between the family members. Many of the negative reactions from your caregivers may have come about through impulsive overreactions and faultfinding, rather than their ability to search for understanding and listen with a caring attitude.

As early as five years old, Rose had memories of her mother's statements that brought blame, guilt, and shame. As a young child, Rose was told to watch after her younger sister while her mother would work around the house. When the younger sister hurt herself the mother would say statements like, "You are worthless. Why didn't you watch your sister?" or statements like, "If you would've been watching your sister like you were supposed to, this would not have happened!" Over the years, Rose would hear statements like, "I don't know why you were born." When the mother became frustrated at the children, she would turn to Rose and say, "I'm sending you to your aunt's house. I can't take you any longer!" Rose never felt accepted by her mother. She felt rejected and abandoned emotionally, and believed it was all her fault. The shaming words of her mother cut deep into the heart, mind, and, soul. Throughout her life Rose never could stop feeling guilty over the smallest of issues. She constantly would apologize for issues that happened, even if she had little to do with the problem. Rose became extremely afraid to express her thoughts and feelings, believing they were never good enough. She was also afraid that expressing her thoughts or feelings would make matters worse, so she believed it was best to remain a person without feelings or an opinion.

Comparisons and expectations

When shame took place in the form of comparisons or performance, the words cut you like a sharp knife. Statements like, "You'll never amount to anything." "You talk like a baby." "Why can't you be like your sister?" would cut to the core. You began to judge and doubt yourself with the thought, "If what I say and do is not right, then I must not be right." If you heard your caregiver or spouse repeat these statements over and over, you began to believe it. You began nonstop messages in your mind like, I'm dumb, I'm stupid; I can't do anything right; I'm not as good as my sister, my thoughts and feelings are not good enough. You judged yourself about everything and began the destructive, self-defeating thoughts and behaviors that kept you in bondage to a shame nature. You did not realize how the words and actions of others influence your self-worth.

I can vividly remember my fifth grade teacher looking at our class with her stone-cold face that would send shivers up my spine. She looked at us with staring eyes and said one day in frustration, "You kids will probably never amount to anything when you grow up." As a ten-year-old child my heart sunk into despair. The butterflies in my stomach increased as I believed she would judge my every word and action. I was afraid to answer questions in class, fearing I would say something wrong. Maybe I won't amount to anything, I thought, as her words rang over and over in my ears. She must be right; after all, she was my teacher. Later in life, I became angry that she insulted me and put me down. I found her words haunting me for years after I left that class.

Caregivers set up expectations by what they say or what they show through their behavior. Those expectations were what you spent your entire life trying to accomplish or measure up to. If you were from a home with frequently changing rules and expectations, you would feel little control over what would happen. You would have a difficult time meeting the expectations, increasing your feelings of not measuring up. This type of home environment greatly influenced your future ability to handle changes in your life. Sam told me that he grew up in a home that was, in his words, "chaotic and out of control." When I asked him to describe his home he said, "You never knew what to expect. The rules always changed." His parents' moods were always changing and you never knew how they would react. Sam became afraid to say his thoughts or express his feelings, fearing his parents would negatively react. The only consistency was the feeling of helplessness, fear, and uncertainty that came from living in the home. Sam realized his constant questioning and doubting of himself was a result of his childhood. As an adult, when Sam felt pulled in too many directions from work, family, and church, he became nervous and felt a sense of helplessness, as if his world was becoming out of control. He later recognized these inner feelings as the same emotional reactions he experienced from the chaotic home of his childhood.

No feelings, no talking about feelings allowed

You may live in or have grown up in a home where feelings were not allowed or not talked about. You learned the household rules about feelings by the examples the caregivers showed through their expression of emotion. They made the rules about what was allowed. Typically, these rules were not very clear and you had to learn by what your parents said to you when something happened. For example, statements like, "There is no reason to cry about it," or "If you don't stop crying, I'll give you something to cry about," tell you that expression of feelings was not allowed. Since your expressions were an extension of how you felt about yourself, the caregivers' negative response to your expressions would give you the belief your emotions were not allowed.

Sherry came to see me wondering why she had difficulty telling others how she felt. She described herself as an emotional person, but she would freeze up whenever she expressed feelings around other people. If she became angry while talking with someone, her emotions would go blank, as if she was afraid to say anything. Sherry described her childhood years as fun and enjoyable. The family was always doing something together. However, she could not think of anything that happened in her childhood that would cause her difficulty with expressing feelings. I asked Sherry to describe the way feelings were expressed in the home. Sherry thought for a moment and with her eyes filling with tears, she said, "I haven't thought about this until now." Sherry continued while wiping her eyes, "I remember when we watched sad movies as a family, I would always hide my eyes from everyone so they could not see me cry." Sherry remembered that she was the only one in the family that showed emotion.

Her parents and siblings always held in what they felt. "I always felt so different, like I was odd. I wanted to be like them." The rule in Sherry's home was not to feel. Since no one else expressed feelings, Sherry believed her crying and expressing feelings was wrong. She was made to feel different from everyone and believed being emotionless was normal. Throughout her life Sherry believed she was not normal and somehow different from the other family members because she expressed emotions.

How the caregivers responded to your expression of feelings gave you the message to determine whether or not feelings were accepted. Comforting statements such as "Come here and sit on my lap," or "You must really be hurting right now. Tell me all about it," showed that feelings were acceptable and the rule that feelings were allowed. Caregivers needed to give adequate attention with words of comfort to provide an encouraging atmosphere for feelings to come out freely. On the other hand, negative responses by the caregiver gave you the message that feelings were not accepted and not allowed. Shameful statements such as, "Stop your crying, you big baby," or "Big boys don't cry," or "What are you crying about now?" or "You need to stop your crying right now, or go to your room," told you feelings were not important and you were not important as well. You may have interpreted these negative statements as saying your feelings were wrong, not needed, stupid, and defective. These messages would discourage you from identifying and communicating feelings, since they seem to either bring negative responses form others or bring feelings of inner pain and rejection.

Another form of the no feeling and no talking about feelings rule may have come from the old belief, "Children are to be seen and not heard." This comes in many types of direct or subtle statements like, "Shut up when I'm talking," or "If I wanted your opinion, I would have asked for it." These statements show little value for your thoughts, opinion, and worth as a person. If your opinions were not good enough, you would believe you must not be good enough. The old notion, do what I say, not what I do, confused the rules and set up a system where you could not win, no matter what you did. The quickest way you learned how to feel was by watching the adults and the consistency by which the adults expressed their feelings. If you heard the no feeling and no talking about feelings messages long enough, you would internalize the belief that feelings were not accepted and should not be expressed. This belief would become a fundamental belief for you. As a result, it may have been difficult for you to be around people who were open with their opinions, and you would continue the same rule in your own family. You may have allowed other people in situations of family, work, church, or community to walk all over you because you had difficulty expressing your own thoughts or feelings.

Minimizing feelings

Caregivers imposed their belief of what should happen to you with statements like, "It's no big deal. There is no reason to be angry," or "There, there, you don't need to cry, it's all right." It's too bad you didn't know enough as a child to say back to your caregiver, "What do you mean don't cry? Can't you see I'm hurting? Why can't I cry if I want to?" The caregiver minimized your opinions, feelings, and ideas, giving the subtle impression that the feelings were wrong, defective, and unworthy.

When I met with Toni she had a very difficult time identifying how she felt. She admitted to getting nervous, having stomach problems, difficulty sleeping, and wanting to run from situations that were upsetting. Toni admitted to never being able to identify her true feelings, as if they were blocked out. She shared that her parents did not talk about their own feelings. It took Toni a long time before she could recall the times her parents often said statements like "Stop your crying. There's no reason to cry over this." Toni initially described her parents as emotionally supportive but later discovered this was not the case when she recalled they rarely encouraged her feeling. Toni interpreted her parents' negative statements that her feelings were wrong and were not to be talked about. She would feel guilty if she expressed her feelings, as if she had done something wrong. Toni realized that she had buried the hurts from the past so deeply, that she had to teach herself how to identify and freely express what was on her heart and mind.

Nonverbal shaming

Another way to create the shame nature is through nonverbal shaming. This subtle type of shame can have a devastating effect and you do not even know it. You may have experienced this through hand or body gestures, facial expressions from others, or through loved ones being emotionally and physically unavailable. Have you ever received the threat of the look from someone as a child or maybe from another adult? It's that cold eyeball stare that penetrates your soul and sends shivers up your spine. It may make you believe you've done something wrong. For others, your parents may have raised their hand or pointed to a belt as a way to threaten you. These acts may create feelings of fear, ridicule, distrust, and a belief you or your feelings are not important. A woman told me that she walked on eggshells at home with her father. Whenever he would show an angry face, she would become instantly afraid that something bad was going to happen. As an adult, she continued this fear whenever someone began to look angry with her.

Emotionally and physically unavailable

Another common type of nonverbal shaming was the times caregivers were not available for you. William Mattox, in his article "The Parent Trap: So Many Bills, So Little Time," Policy Review (Winter 1991, pp. 6-13), found that in 1965 parents spent on average 30 hours a week with their kids. By 1985, parent-child interaction dropped to 17 hours per week. William J. Bennett in his work, The Index of Leading Cultural Indicators: Facts and Figures on the State of American Society (New York: Simon and Schuster, 1994, pp. 102-103), stated teenagers spent only 35 minutes per week talking with their fathers. This shows either a staggering increase in the busy-ness of families or the decrease of value put on raising children. If you only received a small amount of attention from your caregivers, you probably didn't know any difference. Since you had little to compare it with as a child, you never knew what you were missing. You may not have recognized the missed quality love and attention from your caregivers until later in life when you discovered an emotional void or difficulty in feeling love within your relationships as an adult. A caregiver who was frequently away from home was often emotionally unavailable. As a result, it may have become more difficult for you to know how to develop your own emotionally close relationships and learn how to give love and be loved by others.

What would you say if you were asked the question: When you were growing up, did you feel love from your caregivers? If you are like most people I've talk with, you would probably answer, "Yes." How would you answer this second question: What did your caregivers do that showed you love? You would probably tell me how your caregivers worked around the house, bought you something, took you somewhere, watched television with you, or described an activity. Once you listing activities done with your caregivers, I would ask you these questions: Did your caregivers show you love with warm, comforting hugs and kisses? Did you frequently hear reassuring and praising comments like, "You're doing a great job, keep up the good work," or "I love you"? Did you receive gentle and warm hugs and kisses for no reason? When you were hurting, did your caregiver spend time comforting you and allow you to cry and talk about what you felt inside? Did you know what it felt like to feel safe when you are hurting with the comfort of a caregivers arms tenderly wrapped around you while you heard gentle words like, "Tell me where it hurts," or "I'm here with you. Everything will be all right." If you are like the people I've spoken with, the answer to most of these questions would probably be "No." Although good memories are important, did you feel inner warmth from your caregivers' words and actions? Chances are your caregivers tried to love you through their activities, but may not have known how to share the gentle, reassuring love you needed. Chances are your grandparents were also emotionally or physically unavailable to give the love that your caregivers needed. If you did not often hear or feel the caring words or actions previously mentioned, you probably did not recognize what you were missing. Consequently, the less your caregivers showed these gentle and reassuring examples of a caring and loving relationship, the less likely it is you would know how to develop close, emotionally caring relationships in your life.

Approval based on accomplishments

Another nonverbal shame was when your attention and feelings of approval were based on accomplishments. For example, this was especially true with caregivers who may have been physically unavailable and/or you had the responsibility of taking care of another family member, taking care of the house, or other demanding responsibilities. You may have interpreted the caregiver's love and attention was based on the amount and quality of your accomplishments. Although you should never have needed to earn your love, you never knew anything different. Finding acceptance through accomplishments might have been what you believed would get you the attention and approval your heart desired. The caregiver's response to your work was important to how you felt about yourself. If you received a negative comment or no comment at all about your accomplishment, those responses were translated that your work was not good enough. This would often be internalized into the belief that you were also not good enough. Your natural tendency to want approval would drive you to take on more work and try harder in the hopes of receiving the attention and approval you so desperately desired. This created the belief your work was not good enough no matter what you did. You just kept working harder, believing you needed to do a better job, not realizing your caregivers probably did not know how to give the attention you needed. If you could not measure up to your caregivers with what you tried to accomplish on your own, the belief was created that you were not good enough. This belief transferred into other issues of self-judgment about your thoughts and emotions, and the belief that it was safer to work harder and keep silent about what you were feeling.

As an adult you may have continued to find approval through accomplishments. As a result, you would frequently take on more and more tasks at home, work, and church as a way to obtain acceptance. Saying no was too difficult, believing you might hurt someone's feelings or be rejected. You would rarely tell someone how you really felt about the task for fear of losing what little attention or approval you might obtain. Besides, being asked to work was a way to become accepted and strive to be good enough with the people around you. Your never-ending drive to become good enough through accomplishments kept you working harder for the sake of finding approval rather than working for the sake of personal talent or enjoyment in life.

Silent treatment

Other nonverbal hurts may come from silent treatments. If a caregiver did not know how to (or was afraid to) deal with a problem, the easiest way was to not deal with it at all. As a child, your young mind would not understand the silence from your caregiver, interpreting it as a sign that you were to blame. Repeated silences would bring confusion, self-blame, guilt, unworthy feelings, and the belief that expressing feelings was not allowed. You may have continued this self-judgment thinking when you received the silent treatment from others later in life. When Ed came to see me he told about his experiences with his parents. If his parents had an argument they would stop talking to each other for anywhere from several hours to a few days. When Ed had a disagreement with his mother, she would stop talking, leaving young Ed with confusion and self-blame. As an adult, Ed realized in counseling that he was never allowed to adequately express his feelings and had no idea what to do when there was silence or arguments with others.

Physical shaming

Physical shaming can be found in forms of direct physical contact toward you such as hitting, slapping, pinching, shoving, burning, slamming doors, throwing objects, etc. This can also include forcing you to perform unkind acts against your will or when material things, personal care, privileges, or promises are used as bribery, withheld, taken away, or used against you for unkind purposes.

When you were being physically hurt or threatened by a caregiver and not allowed to express your feelings, you would easily feel confused and would quickly shut down emotionally. For example, if a caregiver slapped you, the natural response was to have a feeling of pain, which in turn would bring tears. If the caregiver threatened, "If you don't stop crying I will give you something to cry about," you would force yourself to stop the tears (especially if you experienced this before). The scary message told you crying was bad and you were wrong for showing any feelings. In addition, you developed confusion between the physical pain and the ability to express yourself. You had little choice but to shut down your feelings to survive the pain. If these threats were severe, your mind would separate your emotions from your physical self as a means of coping. This separation became a way of life when you lived in a home with repeated emotional and physical threats and abuse.

Ned told me the sad story about the beatings he would receive from his father. When he first started counseling he showed no emotion when he told about his father making him go out to the back yard to find a tree branch to beat him with. Ned told of the places he thought about to help stop him from feeling the unbearable pain. He only survived by forcing himself to shut off his feelings and think of something else. After many sessions Ned recognized how he separated his emotions from his mind in order to survive. He noticed his emotions became numb while his body would go through the motions like a robot in order to physically get through the crisis.

Like many people who have experienced severe physical trauma, there can be an experience of separation between the mind and body, like you become two people. It has been described in many forms such as, "My inside and outside are two different people," "My emotions are some-where else," "When I feel, I don't know who I am," "I feel like my child takes over when I get upset," "I'm a different person when I'm by myself." (If the abuse is extremely hurtful in childhood or happens over a long period of time, you often cannot remember the trauma.) Since you would look up to your caregiver as someone who was to give you care, you be-lieved they loved you and would not harm you (you did not know the meaning of love). For example, if your caregiver yelled and spanked you for reasons you didn't understand, you would tend to interpret the caregivers' words and punishment as if you did something wrong. Even if you were innocent, you would believe you deserved the punishment, since you didn't know any better. As this type of shaming continued you created the belief that whatever happened was your fault. Since you could not understand why you were to blame, you believed there must have been something inherently wrong with you. If this type of treatment continued, you would carry a deep-seated belief that you were at fault when things went wrong, or you might become hesitant to try new activities, for fear that something would go wrong.

As an adult, if you asked your caregivers if they said or did any thing that shamed you during childhood, they probably would not remember much (if any). If they were raised in shame, chances are they would not recognize that each shaming statement or act was slowly chipping away at your heart, mind, and soul. Imagine yourself using an ax to slowly chop away at the base of a mighty oak tree. Chop after chop, cut after cut, the tree began to develop deeper and deeper wounds. Finally, after enough of the tree was chipped away, the base of the tree would weaken. Unable to stand tall, the deeply wounded tree would fall to the ground. The same is true after each hurting statement or action that chipped away at your heart; you experienced deeper and deeper emotional wounds. Like many people growing up in shaming homes, you could not compare with other homes to know any difference. You believed this type of hurtful, shaming treatment was normal. You believed your caregivers, since they were supposed to be taking care of you and your young innocent mind did not know anything different. As a child you believed your caregivers were supposed to love and protect you. So you thought to yourself, "Why would they hurt me if they loved me?" The only thing you could figure out was that you must have done something wrong to deserve the treatment. Since you could not figure out what went wrong, you believed there was something wrong with yourself. You rarely questioned the authority of your caregivers and you may not have known that your life could have been any different. When you did become aware that your caregivers might have been wrong for what was happening, you either did not know what to do or were too afraid to do anything about it.

Adults shaming adults

It is important to acknowledge that children are not the only ones who can be hurt by shame. Adults are often victims of verbal, nonverbal, and physical abuse, or shaming acts from other adults. As an adult, you may find yourself in an unhealthy relationship with your spouse, family, friends, or associates at work and church. These unhealthy relationships can have the same destructive results of shame that were previously described with children. If you are in an unhealthy relationship, chances are you were in an unhealthy relationship as a child. You tend to continue childhood patterns of behaviors and feelings with people who have similar emotional responses and behaviors. You would often become more comfortable with adult relationships that you were familiar with in your childhood. As odd as it may sound, you would relate more easily to someone who had behaviors you were accustomed to dealing with. For example, childhood feelings of shame were what you learned to expect from other adults. You learned to adapt and become safe with hurtful statements. Anything different, like praise, would be foreign and you would not know how to react (that is why compliments make you so uneasy). You became so accustomed to the feelings of shame, you tended to become involved with relationships that produced similar hurting feelings in yourself. As a creature of habit, you would react to adult situations in whatever way you had learned to deal with them in the past. For example, if your childhood reaction was to leave the room in order to get away from the yelling matches between your parents, then you may have an urge to get away from similar circumstances with adults. When you were a child, the arguing created nasty feelings that were most likely pushed deep inside. If you did not learn to react differently, you would most likely repeat the same behavior until you decide to take control of those feelings. The more you learn about shame, the more hope you will have to stop the repeated cycle of destructive behaviors and emotions.

A woman came to my office stating that most of her life had not been enjoyable and it was hard to do simple things like make friends or say "no" without much guilt. She had to search for some time to acknowledge the feelings of bitterness, anger, and hopelessness which she had for many years after her husband died. Many of those feelings had recently escalated, with bouts of crying and anxiety attacks. The husband was described as demanding and controlling, giving little emotional or physical support. He frequently made cutting remarks to the woman as if she could never do anything right. The frequent verbal put downs created within her a belief that she was not good enough in what she tried to accomplish. Since the husband was emotionally unavailable and would often not let her pursue interests outside the home, the woman focused her life on the children for affection, love, and a sense of purpose. The husband reinforced the no feeling and no talking about feelings rule in the home, and she found herself developing survival techniques of avoidance behaviors to shut out the daily barrage of cutting words. In order to endure, her mind became numb to help survive the years of emotional pain.

She talked about the first few years of marriage with growing signs of a controlling and domineering behavior that subtly became part of the husband's routine. To survive, the woman began giving more and more attention to the children. The desire to maintain a peaceful home environment for the sake of the children was the primary reason she was willing to endure the husband's abusive words and behaviors. Years later she began to realize how the constant verbal belittling, cutting comments, and constant questioning had destroyed her own feelings of self-worth and confidence. She came to realize that the nature of her abusive, insecure husband was to keep her feeling worthless, which kept him in control. The effects of feeling worthless eventually brought her feelings of helplessness and utter hopelessness. This led her to the belief that no matter what she did, it was not going to be right.

As the woman reviewed her life she became angry that she was treated this way, feeling helpless against her husband who inflicted the pain and suffering. The years of suppressed hurt and anger turned into bitterness, resentment, and depression. These feelings consumed her, making life difficult to enjoy. By the time she came into counseling she admitted to a sense of being emotionally dead inside. She regretted the years of suffering and never understood why she married a man who would be so hurtful. Although she always believed her caregivers were caring and helpful, she began to realize her parents were emotionally unavailable, which made her migrate toward similar, emotionally unavailable, adult relationships. She began to understand how adult relationships similar to those in her childhood continued the cycle of unhealthy behavior patterns which was all that she was accustomed to experiencing. This cycle made her more susceptible to hurtful relationships. With the strength of God the woman began to let go of the suppressed emotions, break the bondage of destructive thoughts and behaviors, and begin to love herself for the first time.

You may have a deep sense of feeling defective, unworthy, undeserving, and not good enough. One day you may feel good, be able to accomplish tasks, and believe you can keep going with little problem. The next day you may be full of doubts and you believe you can do nothing right. Or you may have a constant struggle each day with what you believe about yourself. Regardless of what you are going through, your struggle with good and bad feelings has probably been going on for so long you believe it is normal to feel and react that way. It is not normal! This is the result of shame in your life. You can break free from the struggle! You do not need to struggle with these roller coaster emotions. You are allowed to do something with your feelings rather than letting them do something to you. The no feeling rule is not correct and no longer applies to your life. God did not plan for the feelings that He created to be locked away for no one to see or hear. The only way for you to be respected by others is to first identify and respect your own feelings and realize you are allowed to let others know what you feel. You do not need to be shamed by hiding how you feel. The years of verbal, nonverbal, and physical hurts that you buried deep inside become emotional memories that do not go away on their own. The hurtful memories fester within your heart and mind and greatly influence your emotional and physical struggles until the hurts are let go. Your feelings are the key to letting go of the destructive thoughts, behaviors, and deadly bondage created by the shame nature. The chapters ahead will provide valuable information about ways to break free from the bondage of shame.

PS: Words of encouragement

You may have realized for the first time that you were shamed. You probably have all sorts of feelings whirling around inside like a nest of disturbed hornets. You are allowed to have those feelings of hurt, anger, bitterness, and sadness. You are allowed to get those feelings out through tears, talking to God, or talking to a trusted person. You must give yourself permission to talk out what you have learned and let out what you feel inside. You must remind yourself that regardless of what anyone said or did to you, you are good enough. God made you and He does not make junk. God does not make mistakes – people make mistakes through bad choices. Unfortunately, you received hurts from other peoples' bad choices. You have come a long way down your road of healing. This is a rocky part of that road, but don't give up! Don't forget, you are on the road to healing!

> *To you, O Lord, I lift up my soul; in you I trust,*
> *O my God. Do not let me be put to shame, nor let*
> *my enemies triumph over me. No one whose hope is in*
> *you will ever be put to shame but they will be put to*
> *shame who are treacherous without excuse.*
> (Psalm 25:1-3)

Chapter 5

Religious Shame

The Lord is close to the brokenhearted and saves
those who are crushed in spirit. A righteous man may
have many troubles but the Lord delivers him from them all.
(Psalms 34:18,19)

How the image and authority of God were presented in your home, church, and community had a major part in shaping your thoughts, emotions, actions, and reactions concerning God. When the truth about God and His Word was distorted, misused, and abused, religious shame was the result. Religious shame cuts deeper than wounds already experienced from a shame nature. This shame penetrated into the heart and soul like salt poured over an open wound, which greatly affected your ability to identify and feel true emotions. Since religious shame is a widely controversial subject, this chapter will primarily focus on how this type of shame affects self-judgment, denial of feelings, wounding of your soul, and destruction of healthy relationships – especially with God.

What is religious shame?
Plain and simple, religious shame is when caregivers, family, neighbors, and church officials use religion as a means to gratify their own needs, justify their own behavior, mistreat you out of their spiritual misunderstanding of God's Word, or mistreat you because of behavior patterns con-

tinued over the generations. One of the dangers that come from religious shame is how it cuts to the soul and deepest level of the shame nature, destroying the core beliefs about yourself and your ability to have a meaningful relationship with God. The result of religious shame produces an image of God that represents punishment rather than loving guidance; obedience from fear rather than respectful obedience; someone not approachable rather than an accepting God; and an unforgiving God rather than a forgiving God. How God was portrayed in your childhood often influences what you believe as an adult. Think about how you experienced God while you were growing up. Did you hear that God expected little children to behave a certain way, or else? Did you experience God through the words of a preacher saying you would go to hell if you did not act a certain way? Did you experience God from parents who acted one way in church and differently at home?

Children are very perceptive when it comes to watching the behavior of others. I hear stories that describe the confusing and contradicting actions of people when they are not attending church. One man shared that his father was a very respected leader in the church who lived two different lives. He never knew which was his real father. He regularly watched his father gently touch and pray with people in front of the church on Sunday. At home, his father easily became angry, frequently yelling and hitting during punishments. "Spare the rod, and spoil the child" is what the father would say. The scripture was distorted to justify his physical and emotional abusiveness. Ultimately, the child suffered shame, which destroyed his ability to believe in himself and his ability to have trustful or meaningful relationships with other adults or God.

As a child, you may have come to believe God was like the super police, watching whatever you did on His mega TV screen. Did you fear God as someone who at any time could wave His hand, sweeping down to inflict pain and punishment? Or did you picture God calling on a million angels to rush down and rescue you from your problems? Did you become confused about God when you could not find any answers? Confusion about God was made worse with either a gnawing fear that God was waiting for you to mess up or you didn't feel like you could have a good relationship with Him. These fears and beliefs were the result of misconceptions and distortions implanted by people over the years. It is time you learned the truth, to break the destructive patterns of thinking that have kept you in bondage to religious shame.

Misuse of authority

Some people use their position and authority in the name of God as a means of power over others. Church officials can use their power to label, control, belittle, mislead, or abuse (spiritually, sexually, emotionally, or mentally). People can be at a vulnerable point when seeking solace from a church. In addition, when church leaders use religious jargon or scripture references, people are helpless to their authority and suggested influence. It is difficult for an unsuspecting, religiously unknowing person to question the authority of the church – especially when it is a quote from God out of the Bible.

The good news is misuse of authority is the exception rather than the rule. It would be easy to find a respectable church leader willing to listen and guide you in the right path. If your gut tells you something just does not seem right, seek more than one opinion regarding a tough spiritual issue. You can test those gut reactions with the following: 1. Prayer, "Do not be anxious about anything, but in everything by prayer and petition, with thanksgiving, present your requests to God" (Philippians 4:6). 2. God's Word, "Your word is a lamp to my feet and a light for my path" (Psalm119: 105). 3. Godly instruction from someone wiser than you, "Listen to advice and accept instruction, and in the end you will be wise" (Proverbs 19:20).

Not good enough for God

If you were already told you were not good enough or felt not good enough from your caregivers, then you would wonder if you were good enough for God. You thought to yourself, "Why would God accept an unworthy person like me?" "I'm such a failure for everyone else, why would I measure up to what God wanted?" You believed a relationship with God was only for those that were perfect, or at least deserving. Since you believed you were neither of those two things, you would be too afraid to put much effort into a relationship. You would not want to pray, believing God didn't have time for your requests (especially if you felt He was too busy helping more deserving people).

The belief that you were not good enough for God was even more confirmed when you did not feel God answered your prayers; when you did not feel His presence; when you could not perform religiously because you were told God (or the Holy Spirit) wasn't in you; when you were told God (or the Holy Spirit) was not in you because you did not have enough faith; or when you were told you were sick because you were a sinner. The list could go on and on with religious reasons why you were not good enough to get close to God. If you already believed you did not measure up to God's standards, you would be more sensitive to these expectations that would make you feel like the door was closed to acceptance from God. If you were that bad, you wondered how a perfect God could forgive someone like you. You thought to yourself, "I'm not good enough for God to forgive me. I probably wouldn't be allowed into heaven anyway." You believed your true feelings were not good enough for God. Besides, you believed God would not have time for undeserving people like you. You believed holding in your feelings was the best way to keeping peace. Letting out your feelings only made people mad, made you get hurt, and made you feel out of control. You especially did not want that to happen with God. You would believe the poor relationship and experiences with your caregivers would be the same with God. As a result, you believed trying to express your needs in a relationship with God would be too difficult.

When religious adults could not handle situations with you, they began calling on God as if He was the super police ready at any time to come down and handle what they could not. For example, statements like, "God will get you for that!" or "Would God want you to do that?' or "God is not pleased with you!" portrays God as someone to fear – as if God were the one who should be disciplining you. Your caregivers must have forgotten or were never told that God gave them the responsibility to raise you. God entrusted your caregivers to be your teachers on this earth to individually guide and nurture you toward the correct ways of living. Caregivers misusing the authority of God to make up for their lack of knowledge or inability to handle a situation was religious shame. As a result, your caregivers were putting themselves in the place of God. In your mind, all you heard was, God doesn't love you and doesn't believe you're worthy. If you heard these types of statements often enough, you would believe that your thoughts, feelings, and prayers were not good enough for God.

Fearing God

Your childhood concept of God was based on personal experiences of what you saw and heard at that time. The statements of church officials and caregivers played a major part in forming your concept of God and whether He was someone you could trust enough to have a close relationship. You may have imagined God as an all-knowing and all-powerful force high above the skies as He watched your every move. Since you never saw Him, you were always unsure what He was doing or thinking except from what you were told. Depending on your religious background, you were told that if you committed a sin God would send you to hell, strike you dead, cut your tongue off, curse you, strike you down with lightening, or take someone away. Without a true understanding of these statements, they only added to your fear of God.

You may have been scared into submission by believing God could inflict punishment anywhere, anytime, and without warning. Caregivers may have used the fear of God like it was a stick to whip you into shape. They may have used fear as a replacement for the relationship they never were able to establish with you. Or caregivers may have continued the generational belief that obedience was accomplished through unhealthy fear, rather than a healthy relationship. Caregivers who created relationships with fear were often insecure and did not know how to establish a loving relationship to teach obedience out of love, respect, and responsibility. As a result, obedience was from the fear of hurtful consequences, rather than from the hurt you may feel from disappointing the people that love you very much. Your respect and obedience should come as a result of the love and respect that was taught to you. Respect was something that needed to be learned, not forced down your throat like a threat.

An unhealthy fear of God could have been passed down from generation to generation where it was used as a means of discipline. As a result, the focus is on the authority of God from a fear of punishment standpoint rather than learning about a loving relationship with God where respect and obedience are the result of that relationship. From a healthy perspective, having fear of God is beneficial to keeping you on the morally right path. "The fear of the Lord is the beginning of wisdom, and knowledge of the Holy One is understanding." (Proverbs 9:10). The bounty of scriptures in the Bible refer to fear more as a form of reverence and ultimate respect for doing what is right, rather than as a fear to scare you into an unhealthy and hurtful submission. The fear of not wanting to disappoint God is a healthy form of obedience in order to follow what God believes is the best for your life. Anything less than what He wants for your life would be considered second best. "Therefore, everyone who hears these words of mine and puts them into practice is like a wise man who built his house on the rock. The rain came down, the streams rose, and the winds blew and beat against the house; yet it did not fall, because it had its foundation on the rock [Jesus Christ]" (Matthew 7:24, 25).

Healthy fear of God allows you to let the Holy Spirit work on and in the thoughts of your mind. That is called conviction, where your conscience (or mind) would question or bother you enough to the point you would believe something must be done to change or correct whatever you did. Fearing or reverencing God is expected to keep you on the morally right path that God desires for your life. "For I know the plans I have for you, declares the Lord, the plans to prosper you and not to harm you, plans to give you hope and a future . . ." (Jeremiah 29:11,12). God never intended you to be afraid of Him as your Heavenly Father. Instead, He wants you to fear the consequences of anything you do that would be against His plan for your life. Although our hardships and hurtful times of life are the best learning experiences, as a Heavenly Father, God would prefer you not have to learn about life from hurtful experiences. But He knows life will be full of difficulties on a daily basis. Since God gave you freedom of choice, you can make the decision to follow your own worldly pursuits or follow what God believes is best for you. What you choose to do may not be the same as what God believes is the best for you. What God desires for you is written out in His Holy Word. If you do not follow God, you will follow someone or something else. "Do not be deceived; God cannot be mocked. A man reaps what he sows. The one who sows to please his sinful nature, from that nature will reap destruction; the one who sows to please the Spirit, from the Spirit will reap eternal life" (Galatians 6:7,8).

Earthly father and Heavenly father

Think about the authoritarian figures (especially males) in your past. Could you tell them your secrets? Were you able to feel warm inside when you had one-to-one talks together? Would you consider them close friends? Were they emotionally or physically available when you needed them the most? Did you trust them with your life? If the answer was "no" to most or all of these questions, chances are you have a frustrating time trying to develop a close relationship with God. I have found over and over with the people in my office that the relationship you had with your earthly authority figures would be very similar to the relationship you are trying to have with your Heavenly Father. You learned how to have relationships from watching and experiencing the relationships you had with your caregivers. If you had an emotionally unavailable father who was not accessible to hear your sorrows, chances are you have difficulty telling your Heavenly Father what you feel inside. If your father physically and emotionally hurt you, chances are you have a hard time allowing God to become emotionally close and trusting what He has planned for your life. You could have many of the same fears with your Heavenly Father as you did with the other authority figures in your life.

The shame received by your caregivers may continue with God. If you believed you did not measure up to the expectations of your caregivers, you may find it difficult to measure up to the expectations of God. People would say to me, "God is not like my father. Why would I act the same toward Him?" You may respond the same with God as you did with other authority figures as long as you did not learn any differently. How you received love, gave love, trusted, obeyed, feared, and expressed yourself may be the same with God unless you choose to be different. The state of fear that immobilized you from expressing feelings with your caregivers may continue with God. You may have been afraid or did not know how to feel any differently than what you have known for years (this will be discussed in the chapter, "Gauging Your Feelings"). You cannot blame yourself, or God, for what happened in the past. However, you can decide to make changes in your life now, to help overcome the damage caused by the past.

Patty was wiping the tears from her eyes as she described the rejection from her father. The little amount of time he was home, Patty tried to initiate activities with little success. "I wanted a relationship with my dad, but I never had one." She continued, " I never felt good enough for him, no matter what I did." Patty was devastated when her father died suddenly as she became a young teenager. She was emotionally devastated that she could never have the relationship with her father that she always longed for. In order to survive the pain of rejection and abandonment, Patty stuffed the feelings inside. "I blocked out the pain," she said to me. As a young adult, Patty accepted Jesus Christ into her heart while attending church. As the years went on, she began to feel there was something missing with her relationship with God, as if there were a brick wall preventing her from becoming close. In her mind, Patty knew just what to do for a relationship with God. She would continue going to church and reading the Bible, but she could not feel the closeness that she longed for.

During counseling, Patty realized it was difficult to have close relationships in her life, as if there were something blocking her from becoming emotionally close. Patty realized she rarely felt as if she were able to please her parents. She remembered receiving little praise from her father, even when she tried to do her best. In her teenage years her father suddenly died. The trauma from her father's death was so painful, it was as if she would not allow herself to get close to anyone, in fear that she would be hurt again. Patty later realized that she felt shame and rejection from not being good enough for her father, in addition to the abandonment from his subsequent death. She finally realized her past hurts blocked her ability to develop close relationships. Patty learned how to let go of her pain and begin to allow others into her life.

Distorting God

When you were told something enough times by your caregivers, you began to believe it. This was especially true if someone in authority told you statements that distorted God's desires for your life. Distorting God's truths shamed your beliefs and emotions. It destroyed your belief that you were allowed to feel and express yourself with God. You were shamed into believing your thoughts, feelings, and emotions were not good enough for God. The following statements are some examples that distort what God wants for your life.

- **If you use feelings you are not relying on God**. This statement made you believe that feelings were wrong and you were somehow denying the power of God when you expressed feelings. Or, you were made to feel weak and disobedient because you were not relying on God. The truth is, God created you with the ability to feel and express emotions. The Bible is full of examples that illustrate Jesus, the Son of God, expressing feelings (the chapter, Allowing Yourself to Feel, will further illustrate this). Since you can easily be misled by the negative emotions of the moment, God would not want you to rely only on feelings when you are making decisions. For example, I have heard people say, "Why did God leave me, when I needed Him the most?" or "I feel so alone, why did God leave me?" The scriptures are clear that God is always present. "...As I was with Moses, so I will be with you; I will never leave you nor forsake you" (Joshua 1:5). "...And surely I am with you always, to the very end of the age" (Matthew

28:20). As you have read throughout this book, expressing feelings is of the utmost importance for your total well being of mind, body, and soul. However, your decisions should be based on the never failing, never changing Word of God, before you allow the always changing ups and downs of feelings to be the deciding factor.

- **Christians don't get angry.** Have you ever felt that you were not a Christian because you became angry? Or God would be displeased with you because you were angry? The truth is, God knows you have anger, because He created you with it! In fact the Bible gives many references to anger. "In your anger do not sin. Do not let the sun go down while you are still angry, and do not give the devil a foothold" (Ephesians 4:26, 27). God gives you permission to express your anger with strings attached. For example, although anger is allowed when you have been wronged, the Bible makes the point that you must not allow the anger to fester and become an opportunity for it to turn into something you will regret. "Get rid of all bitterness, rage and anger, brawling and slander, along with every form of malice. Be kind and compassionate to one another, forgiving each other, just as in Christ God forgave you" (Ephesians 4:31, 32). Do not let your anger make you hurt anyone else and do not let your anger continue long enough for it to consume you. Even though God expects you to be loving and compassionate toward one another, He never intended you to become a doormat to someone else's ridicule and insults. God gave you permission to feel and express those feelings. Do not let the festering of feelings overcome you or hurt someone else. And do not allow negative feelings to get in the way of enjoying life and developing fruitful relationships with others.

Damage to your soul

To help you understand the inner devastation you experience with religious shame, let's look at the definition of the soul. W. E. Vine in Vine's Expository Dictionary of the New Testament Words (Mclean: MacDonald Publishing, p.1077), defines the soul as, "the breath of life, ...invisible part of man, ...the seat of the personality, ...the sentient element in man, that by which he perceives, reflect, feels, desires." When you experience religious shame, what you perceive, reflect, or feel about your life is distorted. You may say, "Why is there a reason to live? Even

God doesn't want anything to do with me." You begin to believe you do not deserve God's Grace. That is His undeserving, unconditional love, and forgiveness that is available to you. "And God is able to make all grace abound to you, so that in all things at all times, having all that you need, you will abound in every good work" (2 Corinthians 9:8).

As you read in the previous chapter, the shame nature affects you like an ax chipping away at the base of a tree. When you add religious shame to your existing shame nature, it is like the tree is put through a wood shredder, grinding up every fiber that exists. Like the tree, your soul is shredded and damaged with religious shame. The inner belief about your own redemption is destroyed, and you believe you are too undeserving and too unworthy to ever achieve the saving Grace of God. There exists a deep void from the barren soul that you cannot seem to fill with good feelings or a relationship with God. You don't believe you deserve a relationship with God and always question your salvation. This results in the judgment that you are destined to be eternally wrong and the belief that your thoughts and feelings are destined to be eternally wrong. You may believe even if you did have feelings they are wrong and there is no use telling God about them. You also may believe that if God did not want to hear about your feelings, then they would certainly be worthless for anyone else.

If you believed you could not measure up to your caregivers and the church officials would not understand because they were too close to God, who could you turn to for help? You may have a deep sense of worthlessness and empty feeling inside that you could not describe. Rejection from your caregivers was hurtful, but rejection from God was more hurtful than you could bear. You put away those feelings because you never knew what to do with them. You wanted a relationship with God but never felt you could measure up to what He expected you to be or do. Even if the opportunity was available to receive forgiveness or acceptance from God, you felt the worthlessness was too deeply embedded to measure up. Besides, even if you did try to have a relationship with God you were afraid you might mess something up in the process of trying.

The best way to reassure yourself not to fail was not to try at all. You might have stayed away from the church or from God as protection from the hurt. You might have tried over and over again at your relationship with God, but never felt it was where it could be. You grieved the fact that you could never feel closer to God and never understood why your attempts failed. Except for what you saw or heard about other Christians, you did not have much personal experience with developing and maintaining a relationship with God. You might have reluctantly given up trying to get close, believing you didn't deserve that type of a relationship. Or you might continue working at the relationship, praying that somehow a breakthrough might take place.

Religious shame attacks you at your very soul, crippling your ability to have the healthy relationship with God that you want and deserve. Unless you break out of the shame nature, you are robbed of the ability to develop a trusting relationship with Jesus Christ that would bring the friendship you long for, comfort you desire, and reassurance of salvation you deserve. You need to realize that you are not to blame for this type of shame. You did not do anything wrong. God wants to have a relationship with you. Jesus said, "But he said to me, 'My grace is sufficient for you, for my power is made perfect in weakness.' Therefore I will boast all the more gladly about my weaknesses, so that Christ's power may rest on me" (2 Corinthians 12:9). You have the choice to break out of this self-destructive pattern of thoughts, feelings, and actions. Now that you know about religious shame, you must take the responsibility and make the changes in your life. Finding out about the past will not change what happened, but it will help you know what changes need to be made in you to overcome how the past affected you. God is ready, willing, and able to help you find that loving, forgiving, intimate relationship you deserve.

The good news is religious shame is the exception rather than the rule. What has happened to you in the past or the information you learned from this chapter should not be used as an excuse for staying away from religion, a church, or a relationship with God. Although buildings, programs, and people can have an influence on your decision to attend a particular church, that should not make up the only reason why you go to church. Religion is about obtaining a personal relationship with God and church is where you should go to worship Him.

PS: Words of encouragement

You learned some things that might have been hard to read. You still cannot believe religious shame happened and how it has affected you. You may have more feelings whirling around inside than you know what to do with. But take courage, God knows you are hurting and what wounds have been festering inside of you. He loves you and does not want you to suffer from the past any longer. God's grace of forgiveness and comfort is meant for you. "Because of the Lord's great love we are not consumed [with suffering], for his compassions never fail" (Lamentations 3:22).

Your shame does not need to consume you any longer. God is looking forward to a closer and more intimate relationship with you. Don't give up, keep reading!

Chapter 6

The results of shame

*Instead of their shame my people will receive
a double portion, and instead of disgrace they
will rejoice in their inheritance; and so they
will inherit a double portion in their land, and
everlasting joy will be theirs.*
(Isaiah 61:7)

As you read in previous chapters, shame perpetuates your belief that you are, among other things, different, undeserving, defective, unworthy, and not good enough. Consequently, it does not matter what you feel or think, since you believe you will be wrong anyway. Shame nature thinking makes you believe your opinions, thoughts, ideas, and talents are not good enough. You shame your own expression of feelings as if letting out your inner emotions will make you weak, less of a person, or somehow prove your unworthiness. Shame nature thinking destroys your freedom to express your thoughts and the feelings that have been given as a free gift by God. Shame alienates your ability to identify and express feelings as a natural part of your existence. Shame makes you believe you do not deserve to accept love from others and makes you believe your love is not good enough to share with others. Shame robs you of your ability to believe in yourself. You continually doubt your actions and are plagued with the fear that you will not be good enough in whatever you try. The feeling of oppression that results from shame hangs over you like the darkness and gloom just before a bad storm.

The devastation that comes from verbal, nonverbal, and physical shaming has the greatest impact on how you feel, think, and act toward yourself and others. This impact robs you of your ability to have meaningful relationships, experience deeper love, experience inner joy, fulfill needs, and express feelings. This chapter will describe how the shame nature penetrates your heart, mind, and soul, making you helpless to self-judgment, fear, disrespect, self-doubt, unable to love, unforgiveness, and oppression.

Self-judgment

One of the most hurtful outcomes of shame is judgment and doubt against your self. This is the type of judgment that makes you feel less than adequate, with the belief that everyone is constantly judging your every word and action. Your outlook on life becomes clouded and you struggle with feeling good about your own accomplishments. You have a hard time believing in your own abilities and difficulty believing in the compliments that come your way. You believe your opinion doesn't matter, so you do not openly speak your mind or make suggestions in public. Even when you do speak up, you believe everyone else's opinion was better than what you would say. You believe your opinion would not make a difference, so you don't bother saying anything. You do not believe you are deserving, frequently putting others first, with little consideration of what you deserve to receive. You struggle with your relationship with God, questioning the security of your salvation. Your moods swing up and down depending on what someone says to you or what problem happened that day. The way you think about life, respond to others, and perceive yourself is all influenced by the self-judgment you think and feel.

How you judge yourself is important to what you believe about yourself and how you believe others perceive you. You believe you do not deserve to be loved, as if you may be defective and unworthy. Self-judgment destroys your belief that you have anything worthwhile to give to others. Self-judgment brings the doubt and self-condemnation that you are not worthy for any meaningful relationship. This may be a reason why it is so difficult to maintain a close relationship with family, friends, and God. You believe no one would want to have a relationship with someone like yourself. One woman, sobbing with large tears coming down her face, said to me, "I cannot make any friends. No one wants to be my friend. Every time I try to make a friend, I believe they do not want me." I asked the woman if any of the friends had told her they did not want to be friends. She said," No, I just know they don't want to be my friend." No amount of argument would convince this woman away from the brainwashing that she received all her life. She perceived she was not good enough, by the years of cutting remarks and hurtful actions that convinced her she was unworthy to enjoy life and have friends. Her beliefs were presumptuous, false accusations, and judgments toward herself. Her beliefs were one big lie. "Through presumption comes nothing but strife, but with those who receive counsel is wisdom" (Proverbs 13:10, New American Standard).

Playing the same destructive messages

Self-judgment statements are like a continuously playing tape recorder similar to an old continuous loop telephone answering machine. The same messages are played over and over again in your mind. Your thoughts and feelings repeat the same self-judgment beliefs that you do not measure up. These are messages of self-judgment, self-doubt, and self-criticism. You cannot do anything without one of these destructive messages coming across your mind and out of your mouth. Since nothing seems to be good enough, you routinely give judgment messages to yourself or to someone around you. For example, whenever someone gives you a compliment, makes a positive comment about something you do, or you think about your own accomplishments, do you think of judgment messages such as, "It was all right, I guess," "I could never do it right," "Other people can do it better"? What you think about after receiving a compliment is generally what you believe about yourself. For example, if someone says to you, "You did a good job on that project," and a negative message about the project comes across your mind such as, "It wasn't that good," or "I messed up on page four" or "I know I could have done better," you are shaming your own accomplishments through shame nature thinking.

What your caregivers or spouse said to you was like a curse that traveled from their mouth to your mouth. The words penetrated your mind and pierced your heart. You began to believe what they said about you. You would tend to repeat what you heard and mimic what you saw in the role modeling of your caregivers. That is the curse you carry into your generation. What you say about yourself or others can be a curse or a blessing.

"Out of the same mouth come praise and cursing. My brothers, this should not be" (James 3:10,11). The curse would travel from generation to generation, destroying lives as it goes. You must make the decision to break the generational curses. Did you like receiving messages by your caregivers or spouse that were hurtful, disrespectful, and shaming? If you did not like how your caregivers or spouse treated you, then why are you continuing to treat yourself the same way? Every time you think or make shaming comments about yourself, you are repeating the very same treatment you disliked when it was done to you. Every time you give a hurtful and shaming message to someone else, you are continuing the treatment that you hated to receive. These are judgment messages that became conditioned in your mind from what was repeated over the years.

As a child you were especially vulnerable to messages that judged your thoughts, feelings, and actions. You were brainwashed into believing that you were defective and undeserving. The messages became so much a part of you that you did not even realize you are repeating the very same shaming messages that you hated receiving as a child. You hated feeling the hurt and pain that shaming messages would bring. But you felt trapped, as if there were nothing you could do about the messages you heard. You had no idea how the repeated negative childhood messages would impact the future of your life. As long as you continue playing the destructive messages, you are allowing the shame to continue. The choice is up to you whether you stop the continuous playing messages of shame and self-judgment.

Disrespect

Disrespect is one of the most subtle and common forms of verbal and physical abuse. Whether you received disrespect from a caregiver, spouse, friend, employer, schoolmate, or church member, you did not deserve what you received. Disrespect chops away at your self-worth, increases self-judgment, and is a common destroyer of relationships. Disrespect dishonors who you are and what you do, giving little consideration to your needs and desires. Disrespect comes in verbal, nonverbal, and physical forms of hurtful messages that have been previously discussed. The damage of disrespect is a subtle form of evil that often slides from generation to generation. If disrespectful words and actions had been your main diet of treatment throughout your growing up or married years, you become numb to the cutting and abusive behavior, allowing disrespect to become part of your daily routine. As a result, you may disrespect yourself with self-judgment statements and allow others to continue to disrespect you. You may become trapped in a daily diet of mind games, put downs, rude comments, and disrespect of needs and desires. As a result, you may believe what you hear and become numb to the hurt. You may hold in thoughts and feelings, believing they wouldn't change or amount to anything.

In counseling Faye stated she did not feel good about herself and struggled to find joy in her daily activities. She remembered days at school where she was the brunt of jokes or an occasional prank. She acknowledged those events were hurtful but there was little she could do about them. Faye remembered her father and mother making remarks about how she looked or about the boys she dated. She again acknowledged those incidents as hurtful, but she again felt there was nothing she could do about them. Faye shared how her husband would make teasing comments about her cooking or decorating the house. When I asked Faye how she felt when her husband made these comments, she replied, "That's just the way he is." I finally asked, " When you were ridiculed, made fun of, or teased, where did all the hurt go? When did Kaye stop feeling inside? After a long pause, Kaye started crying with the quiet answer, "I guess I shut down when no one was there for me." Over the years the disrespectful comments or actions spread hurt and pain into Kaye's life. Kaye tried not to notice as the repeated disrespect wounded her ability to enjoy life.

Disrespect from your spouse

Disrespect from a spouse is one of the most common ways to destroy a relationship. Disrespect by your spouse is shown through ignoring, belittling, or making fun of your thoughts, feelings, and actions. This can be devastating to your emotional well-being and the very foundation of the relationship. When hurtful words or actions are repeated, your trust and confidence in the other person is chipped away. The disrespectful words and actions can slowly build a wall of anger, resentment, and hurt that slowly shut down your emotions. What results is a festering cancerous growth of emotional separation. A woman came to my office enraged at her husband for years of disrespect. She believed the only way to deal with the issue was through filing for a divorce. For years the husband would rarely finish projects around the house, belittle her with comments, look at other women, and frequently work overtime, rarely giving her or the children much attention. She typically did not want to make any comments in fear it would make matters worse. When she did express her feelings, the husband would make fun of her. To survive the emotional pain of disrespect, rejection, and emotional abandonment, she built a wall of anger and hurt, brick by brick. It was unfortunate that the wife had to get to the point of divorce before she was willing to seek professional help for the years of emotional pain.

If you grew up in a home full of shame and disrespect, you may have come to believe this type of treatment was normal. Often you will allow the same disrespectful treatment to continue with a mate when you do not have any other treatment to compare it to. The disrespect from your caregivers had brainwashed you into believing you were not good enough. As a result, you allow disrespect from your spouse, family, employer, or church, believing what they say doesn't really matter. All you are doing is giving others permission to continue to shame you with disrespect. You may ask, "Why would someone find a mate who would make them feel the same disrespectful way they were treated as a child?" First of all, how can you find a mate who will help you feel different if you do not know how to feel any different than how you were treated all your life? A general rule to remember is, you always want what you cannot have, but you will not know what to do with it when you get it! If you received disrespect with unavailable emotional and physical love, etc., in the years growing up, why would you expect to know what respectful, emotionally available love would look or feel like as an adult?

You may say, "My husband has changed for the worse over the years. He showed me love when I first met him." Typically, it is hard to see the telltale signs of disrespect, when you first meet someone. Too often in my office I listen to the despair of a spouse who verbalizes regret for not listening to their own intuition years ago during the courtship of their mate. When you are not accustomed to identifying feelings, your sense of intuition is clouded and you have more difficulty trusting your inner thoughts. During courtship you are typically blinded by young love and driven by the conquer mode. The conquer mode is where you put on your best behavior for the other person. Men are especially good at conquering what they want. Once men get married, they have finished conquering their wife, so they move on to conquer something else. At that point, men begin conquering their job, recreation, and hobbies, believing the marriage will fend for itself. It is very difficult to break away from a disrespectful spouse when you do not know any other way to be treated. You must allow your eyes to be opened to what your spouse is telling you. Since you are a child of God, He never intended His children to be treated with disrespect by anyone, even your spouse. "Husbands, love your wives, just as Christ loved the church and gave himself up for her to make her holy, . . .husbands ought to love their wives as their own bodies. He who loves his wife loves himself" (Ephesians 5:25, 28). "Wives, submit to your husbands, as is fitting in the Lord. Husbands, love your wives and do not be harsh with them" (Colossians 3:18, 19).

Disrespecting yourself

When you are disrespected, what do you say or think about? Do you have self-judging thoughts such as, "Maybe you are right, I am not very good," or "My husband is right, it's always my fault," or "I might as well not say anything since I wouldn't say the right thing anyway," or "I might as well let my child scream at me since I don't want to make him feel any worse," or "There goes my husband yelling at me again. I'll just have to take it, like I always do." Do you give yourself put-down messages like, "How could I be so stupid?" or "I'll never be able to do that," or "I'm never going to measure up," or "I can never make any friends," or "My hair is so ugly," or "I shouldn't let anyone know how I feel." These are messages of self-judgment and disrespect. When you treat yourself as incapable, not good enough, not smart enough, not lovable, and undeserving, you are disrespecting yourself. When you think or say disrespectful messages to yourself, you are treating yourself no differently than the very people you did not like when they treated you with disrespect.

If you received disrespectful and negative comments throughout your life, it would be very common for you to continue the disrespect with self-judgment comments. If you do not feel good about yourself, you may not know how to treat yourself with respect. Since you have been treated like a doormat when others have stepped all over you with hurtful words; all you may know is what it is like to be a doormat. That may be a shock to you, but it must take a shock to help you realize the destructive way you treat yourself. God instructed you to be humble but never a doormat to someone else's hurtful disrespect. You are a child of God, made in God's image. Whenever someone disrespects you, they are also disrespecting what God created.

This may be the first time you heard about disrespecting yourself. Each time you put yourself down, discredit a compliment, believe you could not accomplish something, or doubt yourself, you continue to disrespect yourself. It is easier for others to disrespect you when you do not respect yourself. For example, if someone says to you, "What did you do that for? That was a stupid thing to do," you have two choices to respond. You can disrespect yourself and think, "I guess you are right, that was stupid," or "I can never do anything right." These thoughts automatically assume you are stupid because you decided to do something the way you believed it should be done. Consequently, you would disrespect yourself by allowing that person to call you stupid. Or, you can respect yourself and think, "I believed the task should have been accomplished that way. I am not stupid and I should not be treated that way." Even if the task turned out to be wrong, you could admit to the wrong, but not accept being called stupid. You may say, "I can correct what I did, but I do not deserve to be called stupid. I did not appreciate that comment."

Respecting your feelings

Respecting yourself is very important when it comes to allowing you to express thoughts and feelings. If you have been disrespected throughout your life, not allowing yourself to be honest with your feelings is very common. You would believe your feelings were not important or insignificant to others. God freely gave you feelings to receive your fulfillment of needs and desires. You were given the feelings as a gift to express yourself to others. God is honored when you tell Him how you feel. You are respecting yourself when you express the feelings that God gave to you. Each time you deny your right to express God-given feelings, you are disrespecting your own right to have needs met. If your needs were not met when you were disrespected as a child or with a spouse, you would not believe your needs should be respected later in life. A woman told me once that when you stop having feelings, you become a faceless person, someone without an identity. You lose your identity when you do not allow yourself to express your feelings, thoughts, or opinions.

You previously learned that your feelings were an extension of what you believed and what you needed. When your feelings are not respected, your beliefs and needs are cut at the core. The person disrespecting you is saying, "I don't care about your feelings and I don't care about your needs." When you allow that person to be disrespectful, you are denying your ability to have your needs met. As long as you allow the other person to be disrespectful, you are enabling the unhealthy relationship to continue. If you decide to do nothing about the hurtful comment, you are disrespecting yourself by not expressing what you feel and essentially giving the person permission to continue the disrespect. In essence, you are denying your God-given right and personal need to appropriately express your hurts. If you express your feelings after a hurtful comment and the person disrespects you by making fun of your feelings, chances are the person is probably very insecure about dealing with emotions. If this type of disrespect happens frequently in your life, you may want to receive professional help to learn how to handle abusive people and recognize unhealthy relationships. As this disrespect continues chipping away at your heart, mind, and soul, you will not be able to escape the disrespect until you decide you do not want to be treated that way. Every time you are disrespected as an adult, you are allowing the lifelong destructive messages to continue hurting you. You must take responsibility to respect yourself and not allow others to disrespect you.

Not able to set boundaries in your life

Do you have a hard time saying "No?" Do you say "Yes" when you really want to say "No?" Do you have a hard time letting people know what you need or feel? Do you allow yourself to be a doormat from the rude comments of others? If the answer to these questions is "Yes," you have difficulty setting and respecting your own boundaries. When you respect yourself you are telling others what you believe is important and what you are willing to tolerate. You are setting your boundaries for the type of treatment you are willing to accept. If you allow insults, put-downs, time pressures, inappropriate comments, and unreasonable demands you are allowing yourself to be disrespected. You need to verbalize your boundaries of respect and consideration to make others know where those boundaries begin and end. For example, if your husband, friend, or teenager is inappropriately yelling at you because they are angry, you have two choices. You can allow them to treat you like a doormat by allowing them to yell. Or you can let them know you want to be treated with respect by setting your boundaries. You can say, "You can tell me you are angry, but I do not appreciate you yelling at me. If you do that again I will leave the room until you can speak more calmly." You must take responsibility for setting boundaries with others. You have every right to expect people to take responsibility for their own actions. If they are an adult (or teenager) and do not take responsibility for their own actions, you should not have to put up with their irresponsibility. You have every right to expect the other person to treat you with respectful words and actions.

Not allowing yourself to express feelings will make it difficult to set adequate boundaries in your life. When someone speaks rudely and you feel hurt, in order to set your boundaries it is important to express your feelings of hurt and dislike of their tone of voice. If you are hurt by someone and choose not to do anything about that hurt, you are giving the message, you are allowed to disrespect me and treat me like a doormat. In addition, the suppressed hurt will fester like a cancer growth. At this point in your life you have a dilemma. You may decide to not say anything and let the hurt fester inside, making your life miserable (and miserable for others around you). Or, you can tell the person how much their comment offended you. In theory it sounds easy to just tell someone you hurt. Unfortunately shame nature makes it very difficult to respond to people who disrespect you. You may not respond out of your own feelings of guilt; fear of hurting someone's feelings; fear of rejection; fear of being unspiritual; fear of someone hurting you; or fear of being selfish. Ultimately, shame nature makes you willing to do whatever needs to be done, whenever it needs to be done, for whoever needs it done – at the physical and emotional expense of your own needs. You should respect yourself and set boundaries at home, work, school, and even church. You should be allowed to express your own thoughts and feelings to tell others of your hurts, needs and desires. You should be allowed not to respond to unhealthy demands of others through fear, guilt, pressure, punishment, blame, shame, threats, and unrealistic expectations.

Fear of failure

The shame nature produces self-judgment and the destructive belief that whatever you try will not be good enough or end up as a failure. If you have been questioned throughout your life in everything you try, the message you heard was that nothing was good enough. You became afraid to try something or believe you must defend what you do. Shame produced the belief you were not good enough, not worthy enough, or not talented enough, to try something without it going wrong. On the other hand, you may be afraid to make a decision because you were told in the past, "Don't do this," Don't say that," "Do it this way," "Say it that way." As a child it was important to learn how to safely succeed and fail with caregivers that would lovingly support you no matter what happened. When that did not happen, you may have developed insecurity about yourself or making decisions. The following are some of the ways fear can show up in your life:

- **Procrastination**. You wait until the last minute before the deadline to complete a task. This is not to be confused with simple laziness. As a procrastinator you don't even realize you are afraid to fail. You do not have confidence you will do well on a task. You avoid finishing the task, believing you may not do a good job, something wrong may happen, or someone will criticize the outcome. If you were treated with the expectation that you could never do anything right, you continued to put things off with the underlying fear that what you accomplish may not be right. One man in my office described the dozen unfinished projects around his house. These projects were a major source of conflict with his wife. Whenever his wife became upset about an unfinished project, he would leave the room. During his growing up years, this man had a father who seemed to make a negative comment for everything he tried. As a result, he never felt good about his accomplishments and experienced so much self-judgment, he was afraid to finish his projects. He believed he would never do a good enough job, as if he would never measure up to what his father would expect. The best way to shield himself from his fear of criticism was to avoid talking or finishing his projects. He did not realize the childhood criticisms were the origin of his procrastination and his difficulty to talk about his own feelings.

- **Perfectionist**. You work extra hard making sure everything is just right. This becomes such a way of life you do not realize how hard you work in efforts to be good enough for yourself and everyone else. It is hard to realize that deep inside you never feel like you can succeed. You believe what you do is never good enough, not because of what people tell you, but from what you feel. It is like this little voice keeps telling you to do more in the hope that it will someday be good enough. Unfortunately, no matter how hard you try it never seems to feel like you did it right.

- **Obsessions**. You must have a place for everything and everything in its place before you believe it is good enough. Obsessions are an overwhelming need to accomplish something to help you feel in control. There is excessiveness to many things you do – organizing, checking, cleaning, or tidying. This is not the same as when you must tidy up the house because you just found out company is coming. This is a compulsive and overwhelming need to make sure the house or office is tidy and clean before you do anything. You have a fear that someone will find out you are not good enough, so you work extra hard not to let that happen. You must make sure you are good enough by overcompensating for what you are responsible. You cannot relax or feel right about a situation until you make sure everything is in its place. You may need to check things two, three, or more times because you doubt you did it right the first time.

- **Avoidance behaviors**. This is what was written in the chapter, "Protecting Yourself From Your Feelings." This is when you emotionally react to avoid situations or feelings that you are afraid to experience. You may react as a result of fear generated from situations that are currently happening or from something that you are afraid will happen. Typically, situations from the present are the triggers that dredge up the emotional hurts of the past.

- **Fear to express yourself**. Shame also produces fear that something will happen if you express your feelings. You cannot describe the fear. You only have a sense that something bad will happen if you express emotion. For example, you may fear becoming emotionally out of control, something will happen, or fear people will not like you. You may believe your feelings are wrong to start with and expressing them will only make the situation worse. You may believe expressing feelings would make you a terrible person, or make you vulnerable to more hurt. A woman sitting in my office was describing how her husband would frequently threaten her. In the middle of her description she suddenly closed her eyes and stopped talking, as if to hold back pain. In tears she said, "I don't want to talk about this any more." Feeling the hurt from the past experiences was too scary and painful to continue. Fear is a major destroyer of peace of mind, inner joy, and happiness. Not being good enough drives you to fear and paralyzes your ability to freely express yourself in words or actions. When you do not trust your own judgment and abilities, you become afraid of your own feelings.

• **Defensiveness.** When you repeatedly react to protect yourself from the comments or actions of others. This is not the occasional times you stand up for yourself when someone gives a nasty comment. This defensiveness originates from shame, which produces an underlying insecurity or fear that you will be blamed or be not good enough. As a result, your deep insecurity creates the belief you must constantly defend yourself when people make comments or ask questions.

Giving or receiving love

There are volumes of self-help material on how to fall in love, stay in love, and renew your love. However, if you have been shamed, you do not feel worthy or good enough to be loved. The messages of self-judgment, doubt, and disrespect are destructive and crippling to your ability to accept or give love away. If the relationship with your caregivers was not based on a foundation of love and trust, it will be more difficult to know how to develop loving relationships as an adult. For example, if you did not see examples of love through words and actions, did not receive love, or did not have opportunities to give love, chances are you will have difficulty receiving and giving love later in life. If you did not receive love, you would tend to feel there was something wrong with yourself. In turn, you would have difficulty knowing how to feel good about yourself (love yourself). If you did not love yourself, you would consequently believe you were not good enough to receive love and your love was not good enough to give away. You must love yourself first before you can believe you are worthy enough to let others love you or believe your love has worth for someone else.

If you did not have a loving relationship, comforting physical touches, and kind words, you would not know what you were missing. If you had nothing to compare love to, you would typically interpret love to simply mean the physical presence of a caregiver, the absence of being hurt, or the receiving of material things. As you moved into adulthood, life took on more meaning and you may have begun to realize there was something missing – but you just could not pinpoint the feelings. As you became more involved in relationships you began to search for what you were

91

missing. Some people go from one relationship to another continuing to search for that missing element and never finding it. In essence, you were looking for the love, affection, security, or a sense of completeness that you never obtained from a relationship with your caregivers. Since you did not receive love as a child, you did not know how to receive it as an adult. You would reject someone else's love when you were not accustomed to receiving it, as if the affection made you made you feel uncomfortable or smothered.

I met with a young woman named Ruth, who described herself as having to pursue the emotional affection and attention from her current boyfriend. Since she loved the boyfriend it did not matter that she had to do most of the work to maintain the relationship. Even though Ruth did not receive much initiation of attention from her boyfriend, she was quick to tell me she worked hard to receive love from him. When I asked if she had any other experiences with relationships in the past, she described her first boyfriend. Although Ruth believed her first boyfriend was affectionate and caring, she felt he would get too emotionally close, as if being emotionally smothered by him. Ruth ended the earlier relationship with her first boyfriend because she could not handle him getting too emotionally close.

When I later asked Ruth to describe the relationship with her father, she said he was emotionally cold and distant to all members of the family and provided very little expression of love and feelings. Ruth was the one who had to pursue the affection and attention from her father. Ruth realized her perception of love was in the form of initiating and pursuing a man to receive her emotional needs. She was so accustomed to being the pursuer in the relationship with her father, that she was uncomfortable when she was pursued and shown love and attention by her first boyfriend. She finally realized that she was pursing her current boyfriend since that was what she was accustomed to doing in a relationship. Although the affection from the first boyfriend was the more appropriate and respectful love, that type of a relationship was out of her experience and comfort zone.

Like Ruth, you often learn about relationships from the type of relationships you had with your caregivers. You often migrate toward the expressions of love in a relationship that you are familiar with and within your comfort zone. Since Ruth's father was not expressive with his love, Ruth did not learn how to receive it or give it away. Ruth was shamed into believing she did not have a right to be loved. She did not know what it was like to receive words of love and affection. Ruth's shame was emotionally crippling her chances of having a mutual loving relationship. She did not have an example to teach how to identify her feelings and express her own love. As a result, she continued to disrespect herself by finding emotionally unavailable men and not receive the love she deserved.

Unforgiveness

While working in the medical field for many years, I often heard sad stories where people would visit their doctor for a simple ache in their body – only to receive the shocking news they had some terminal illness with only a short time to live. I would often be asked to counsel with these people who were despondent with disbelief over the diagnosis. In counseling I would hear the familiar story that they always wondered about their persistent ache, but had no idea it was a festering illness growing inside. They never realized how severe the condition could become without seeing the physical telltale signs.

Unforgiveness is very similar to an illness that festers inside. When hurts are buried they do not go away. They take root in your heart and every time you complain about the offense the root grows deeper and deeper. The unforgiveness is like cancer cells that multiply through bitterness, resentment, anger, and rage. As you let these unforgiving feelings continue, you lose control of your mental, physical, and spiritual areas of your life. Drs. Minirth, Meier, Hemfelt, Sneed and Mr. Hawkins, in their book Love Hunger (Nashville: Ballantine Books, 1990, p. 26), state the following: "When we hold resentment against God, others or ourselves, serotonin and norepinephrine are depleted in our brain cells. These are the chemicals that move across the synapses from one cell to the next, the chemicals that we think with, move with. When these are depleted, people lose energy and motivation." Serotonin is the chemical that boosts your mood. The lower the serotonin level, the more depressed your mood becomes.

Unforgiveness and unresolved hurts are like an open wound into your heart, mind, and soul, for problems in your emotional, physical, and spiritual areas of life. Those open wounds can be the entry point for the devil to exercise his evil schemes. As you keep these wounds open, you are giving permission for negative activity to take place within your heart and mind.

You think more hurtful thoughts, feel more hurtful emotions, and experience more physical and emotional problems.

Oppression

Have you ever felt gloomy, like a dark cloud was hovering over you? Have you ever felt the constant weight or pressure of an inner hurt or ache? Have you felt despair inside, like life was not worth living? Is it hard to find real joy in your daily activities? Do you find it hard to spiritually grow, as if something is blocking you from getting close to God? Do you feel emotionally dead inside? Do you feel like it is hard to move on with your life? Everyone may experience a small portion of what has been described. However, if you experience most of the things described, most of the time, you are emotionally oppressed.

Oppression is an outside force that penetrates your innermost being. Oppression is the result of verbal, nonverbal, and physical abuse, and shame that enters your heart, mind, and soul. The shame penetrates your heart and squeezes the very life out of it, like squeezing a handful of soft clay that oozes out between your fingers, depleting any recognizable shape of the clay. In the same way, oppression is when the life is squeezed out of your heart and soul. You feel like there is little hope of having a normal life. You struggle to find purpose in your life. You have a difficult time keeping yourself motivated and interested in long-term projects. Shame and self-judgment invade the soul like an octopus smothering you with its heavy tentacles wrapped around you. You cannot escape the evil clutches of the ugly creature that pulls you down to the deepest part of despair. You struggle to find something good in your accomplishments, only to repeatedly feel defeated in whatever you try. You either give up trying or wait awhile until you try something again, repeating the process of defeat all over again.

It is hard to recognize oppression because you do not realize what it is like to be anything different than the oppressed state you are living in. This is especially true if you have lived in oppression throughout your life. In addition, oppression is not talked about or recognized by most professionals or many churches. Oppression creeps up on you like an evil, slithering snake crawling behind your back. The snake is the best way to describe oppression, because it represents the evil of Satan. You must know that God is aware of Satan's evil. That is why you need God's protection.

"Then your light will break forth like the dawn, and your healing will quickly appear; then your righteousness will go before you, and the glory of the Lord will be your rear guard" (Isaiah 58:8). The world is full of evil all around you. "We know that we are children of God, and that the whole world is under the control of the evil one" (1 John 5:19). You are living in the battleground between good and evil. God wants the best for you, but Satan wants you to suffer. "Be self-controlled and alert. Your enemy the devil prowls around like a roaring lion looking for someone to devour. Resist him, standing firm in the faith, because you know that your brothers throughout the world are undergoing the same kind of suffering" (1 Peter 5:8, 9). On the other hand, God desires you to experience a life filled with abundant love and joy. "If you obey my commands, you will remain in my love, just as I have obeyed my Father's commands and remain in his love. I have told you this so that my joy may be in you and that your joy may be complete" (John 15:10, 11).

Everyone experiences some struggle between good and evil every day. However, when you are oppressed, you cannot be victorious over your daily struggles. You may occasionally win a battle but you always feel like there is a war raging inside. You only feel temporary acts of accomplishments with little feeling of permanent contentment or lasting joy. You remain oppressed because you do not know any difference. That is exactly what the devil wants you to believe. The devil wants you to struggle in darkness and continue in bondage to shame and self-judgment. However, you don't have to continue in this bondage. You can be victorious!

"Put on the full armor of God so that you can take your stand against the devil's schemes. For our struggle is not against flesh and blood, but the rulers, against the authorities, against the powers, of this dark world, and against the spiritual forces of evil in the heavenly realms" (Ephesians 6:11,12).

As you suffer in oppression, you will experience deterioration of physical health. Many physical illnesses can be greatly influenced from emotional stress and trauma, as you read in the first few chapters. When you have little emotional energy to feel good about yourself, you begin to let your physical health deteriorate. You may not take care of yourself as you should. You do not eat right, think right, drive right, feel right, sleep right, and the list goes on. God knows all about oppression and how it affects your heart, mind, and soul. "You know of Jesus of Nazareth, how God anointed Him with the Holy Spirit and with power, and how He went about doing good, and healing all who were oppressed by the devil; for God was with Him" (Acts 10:38, New American Standard). Satan continues to be as evil and ruthless today as he was during the time Jesus walked the earth. However, the power of Jesus Christ is also still as mighty and victorious today as it was in Jesus' day. You do not need to remain captive to the oppression that holds you down and keeps you from the joy that you deserve. You are not alone in your struggles. You are still able to call on Jesus Christ for help with your needs. The next chapter begins the process of becoming victorious in your desire to overcome these struggles.

PS: Words of encouragement

This chapter may have opened your mind and heart to new feelings and thoughts that you never knew existed. You may have received answers to problems in your life. Or you may have created more questions. You may be tired of reading about the hurts and misery you have gone through in the past. Now that you have more information, you may be ready to get rid of the self-judgment, doubts, fears, unforgiveness, and oppression and move on to find real joy in life. It may be scary at first as you begin to express your feelings and change your thought life. The more you express yourself, the more confidence you will development. As your confidence increases, the more layers of shame will fall off.

The Spirit of the sovereign Lord is on me, because the Lord has anointed me to preach good news to the poor. He has sent me to bind up the brokenhearted, to proclaim freedom for the captives and release from darkness for the prisoners.
(Isaiah 61:1)

II

Find healing through your feelings!

Chapter 7

Allowing yourself to feel

My inmost being will rejoice when your lips speak what is right.
(Proverbs 23:16)

If you lived or currently live in a family where feelings are not encouraged, not allowed, or not talked about, chances are you will have little understanding of what feelings are, how to identify them, or what to do with them. It may be common for you to shy away from expressing feelings and become confused, nervous, or want to get away when something evokes some type of emotion in you. You may not like to feel, in the fear that something may happen if you let the feelings out. Joann's face was motionless as she described her husband's angry yelling sprees. "Why are you so stupid? That's not how you do it," he would repeatedly say. During our counseling session I asked, "What do you feel inside when he yells at you?" Joann had a puzzled look on her face as she gazed at the floor. She said, "I don't know. I need to try harder, I guess." Joann had no idea what she felt inside, as if my question was in a foreign language. She later recalled childhood images of her father yelling whenever she expressed feelings. Joann believed it was normal for men to yell and for her to be afraid when she expressed feelings.

For many people I speak with, letting feelings bubble up inside while trying to describe what is happening can be confusing, scary, or overwhelming. The following are some of the questions regularly asked by men and women as they are learning how to express feelings. Am I allowed to tell someone how I really feel? Should I be allowed to express feelings that may show a side of me people may not like? Am I allowed to get angry with someone, especially if I'm a Christian? Will I lose control of my feelings if I let them out? Will I be rejected if I express my feelings? Regardless of how you interpret feelings, you need to understand two important principles: First, you were born with the feelings that God created. It was people in your life that took them away. Second, you should be allowed to express (unless you are forced not to) the feelings God freely gave you as long as they are expressed in a respectful manner. God planned it that way!

Allowing yourself to feel

In previous chapters you read that feelings are a God-given, natural reaction to what is happening around you. Now it is time to give yourself permission to feel. Do not hold back what has been freely given to you. For example, the ache in your stomach after someone yells or after conflict, is your emotional response to the conflict. If you are like many people, the stomach ache, anxiety, numbness, or other inner response has become so common in your life, you have become crippled to do anything about it. God never intended you to be consumed with inner turmoil and not allowing yourself to say what you feel about it. To begin allowing yourself to feel you must first become aware of what is happening inside. You must give yourself permission to identify and say what is physically and emotionally happening inside. For example, when someone yells at you, give yourself permission to describe what is happening inside. If you are hurt, then say how you feel. You may say to that person, "It hurts me when you yell at me." If you cannot directly tell the person what you feel, privately speak it out loud to yourself, write down, or share with a friend, "It really hurt me when that person yelled." Emotional reactions do not have to be negative. When someone close to you gives a hug with the words "I love you," you should feel an inner glow like being wrapped in a warm blanket. "I feel warm inside when you tell me that," you may say. Chances are, many people reading this may not be able to quickly put into words what they are feeling at the time of that emotional experience. That is understandable if expressing feelings was not learned. Allowing yourself to identify and understand what is whirling around inside will begin the process toward freedom of expression. You have a right to express hurtful feelings, when your "gut" tells you something is wrong. Similarly, you have a right to express pleasant feelings when your heart tells you something is right. (The next chapter will provide steps to help you identify and express your feelings.)

The fact that you have feelings is no accident. Your body uses emotions as a basic source of survival. For example, the small holes on the bottom corners of your eyes, called tear ducts, are to wash the eyes for protection and to release tears when you are hurting or laughing. When you are afraid, your brain automatically tells the body to produce adrenaline, giving a boost to either fight the conflict or run away. During times of shock or emotional hurt, your mind can shut down the pain as a form of protection against too much hurt at one time. Your mind and body have been wonderfully made to react to the pleasures or hurts that come your way. God knew what He was doing when He created you. God gave you what was needed to find fulfillment and enjoyment in life. "God. . .richly provides us with everything for our enjoyment," (1 Timothy 6:17). Enjoying life includes the expressions of love, laughter, or tears that accompany our experiences. Enjoying the fullness of life would be impossible without feelings.

Imitating your Heavenly Father

As you have read earlier, you are born with the ability to experience and express feelings. However, there may not have been people in your life who were healthy role models to help you learn how to appropriately identify and express what was on your mind and heart. It is never too late to learn how to express healthy feelings. You need someone who really cares about you and wants to role model healthy ways to deal with emotions. The best role model I know is from what I read in the Bible about the life of Jesus. The Bible clearly tells you to "Be imitators of God..." (Ephesians. 5:1), and God gave you Jesus as the example to imitate. Let's look at some of these examples.

Jesus had a very good friend named Lazarus. When Jesus heard of Lazarus' death He went to the place where he was buried. When Jesus looked around at the people crying over Lazarus' death, "*Jesus wept*," (John. 11: 35) with compassion. It is also believed Jesus was saddened by

101

the people's grief and disappointed that the people could not understand the saving power of the Heavenly Father.

During the Jewish Holy time of year called Passover, it was the custom of the Jewish people to offer, through sacrifice, an unblemished animal to God in order to receive forgiveness of their sins. The temple courtyard was like an open marketplace with merchants (money changers) selling animals such as oxen, sheep, and doves. "So he [Jesus] made a whip out of cords, and drove all from the temple area, both sheep and cattle; he scattered the coins of the money changers and overturned their tables. To those who sold doves he said, 'Get these out of here! How dare you turn my Father's house into a market!" (John 2:15-16). During this situation Jesus revealed His frustration, and showed a rare but clear expression of *anger* toward those who were making a mockery of the church.

In the Garden of Gethsemane, moments before His arrest by the Romans, Jesus prayed alone to God. Jesus was aware of the barbaric treatment and painful death that the cross would soon bring to Him. With a heavy heart and great apprehension of the coming events, Jesus probably knelt while praying, " 'Father, if you are willing, take this cup from me; yet not my will, but yours be done....' And being in anguish, he prayed more earnestly, and his sweat was like drops of blood falling to the ground" (Luke. 22:42, 44). As a physician, St. Luke was able to describe the rare phenomenon that Jesus experienced called Hemathidrosis or bloody sweat. This is where the tiny capillaries in the sweat glands break under tremendous emotional *stress, fear,* or *agony.* Given the horrible experience of dying on the cross that awaited Jesus, His humanness showed briefly through His physical and emotional reactions.

During the sentencing, Jesus stood motionless before the Roman Governor, Pilate, who asked the crowd of Jews what they wanted to do with Jesus. Their reply was, "Take him away! Take him away! Crucify him!... You have no king but Caesar" (John 19:15). There is no doubt that Jesus would feel tremendous *sadness* and *rejection* when His own people shouted to have him taken away to be killed through crucifixion.

Although the disciples became very close to Jesus throughout the three years, they had difficulty understanding and believing His teachings. Toward the end of His ministry, Jesus repeatedly tried to help the disciples with their confusion and unbelief through assurance that when He went away, He would come back again. One day, after much discussion, the disciples finally understood what Jesus was saying. Jesus *joyfully* remarked to the disciples, " 'You believe at last,' Jesus answered" (John 16:31).

As the Divine Son of God and the earthly son of Joseph, Jesus Christ had the ability to experience all human emotions and feelings while living on the earth. Do you want to be "Christ-like" in your heart, mind, and actions? Then you should identify and express your feelings as portrayed by Jesus. If God wants you to be an imitator of Him then it is acceptable to show the feelings He created. Conversely, if you decide to not express your feelings through actions or words, you are not being "Christ-like." God promises that the benefits you receive will outweigh the changes you must make by expressing your feelings. "Whatever you have learned or received or heard from me, or seen in me – put it into practice. And the God of peace will be with you" (Philippians. 4:9). Allow your Heavenly Father to teach what you did not learn from your earthly caregivers.

Letting the feelings out

The physician and author Bernie S. Siegel, MD, wrote in his book, Peace, Love and Healing, (New York: Harper & Row, Publishers, 1989, p. 29), about the significance of releasing all of our feelings. He wrote, "It's important to express all your feelings, including the unpleasant ones, because once they're out they lose their power over you; they can't tie you up in knots anymore. Letting them out is a call for help and a 'live' message to your body." You have read throughout this book how important feelings can be for the well-being of your life. However, you may find expressing feelings is like sitting alone in a stalled car, stranded in the middle of nowhere. You realize there is nothing you can do but sit alone and be helpless until you get the help you need. It is common for you to have great difficulty identifying and saying the feelings that whirl around inside. When you try to feel, your mind may be like a blank movie screen or in total confusion like a movie in fast-forward. You may have a nagging fear that something will happen if you feel. Whatever you experience, it is important to share with a trusted friend or family member what you see and feel inside your mind and heart.

Some people believe the act of showing emotions is through the behaviors of yelling, hitting, running away, not speaking, throwing objects, slamming doors, swearing, loud laughter, cruel words, etc. These are forms of energy release, which may be helpful to get out the negative energy but are not helpful or healthy for yourself or the person on the receiving end. If you would take a step back and replay your actions through a video camera, you would probably (hopefully) be embarrassed by the behaviors you observe. These actions are typically outward explosions of energy from feelings that have been held in to the point of overload. Whenever Julie and Allen had an argument, Allen would walk out of the room, slamming doors and yelling, "I've had enough." In a voice loaded with frustration Julie said to me, "We always get into an argument and before I know it, he's out the door." Allen later revealed that feelings were not allowed when he grew up. He was saddened when he realized he was behaving the same way as his father reacted to his mother years ago.

Take control or be controlled

One basic premise I learned in my high school physics class was that every action has a reaction. This premise also relates to how you react to people or circumstances throughout your life. You react emotionally and physically to whatever someone says or does by the message that is sent. That message can be a great source of energy that fires up emotions like an exploding water balloon that soaks you all over. For example, if someone speaks harshly to you, their tone of voice will create a negative flow of emotional energy inside you, such as hurt, fear, anxiety, etc. Depending what you decide to happen, the negative energy will continue to whirl around inside like an emotional roller coaster. You can decide to either take control of the energy; let it out in a healthy way or decide to ignore the energy and allow it to control you by coming out through unhealthy behaviors.

Let me explain what feelings can do to you. If you choose not to feel by pushing the emotional energy down inside (believing it will stop the emotional roller coaster), you may temporarily stop the flow of emotions on the surface, but the energy will whirl deeper inside until it reacts with an explosion in unhealthy ways. The emotional energy begins to control you when the mind and body cannot hold in any more negative emotions. You begin to experience physical symptoms such as irritability, poor sleep, crying, fatigue, headaches, nervousness, etc. You can be consumed with feeling trapped, hurt, angry, moody, offended, or guilty, with the belief that you cannot do anything about those feelings. You probably do not understand why you feel this way. You become controlled by these feelings and don't even know you can be free from the pain, hurt, drudgery, and oppression that these feelings bring. This is especially true when you were raised in a family where you learned to push down feelings and were not allowed to let the feelings out. If you continue to hold the energy in, you are susceptible to the physical and mental illnesses discussed in the previous chapters.

When the roller coaster of emotions is whirling inside, you can choose to take control. Controlling the emotional energy means the process of first identifying the feeling that you have inside and next, saying what you feel. The emotional energy is released as you identify and express what you feel (the next chapter will provide detailed steps to this process). You now have a choice: you can hold the energy in and wait for it to come out through some unhealthy behaviors or you can decide to release the energy through appropriate feelings. When you choose to release the energy by saying what you feel, you are taking control of those feelings and greatly reducing the potential of an explosion of energy through unhealthy reactions.

Feeling out of control

Among the most common road blocks to expressing feelings is a fear of becoming "out of control" when feelings are let out. The mere thought of letting out feelings can bring a dread that emotions will uncontrollably gush out and take you "over the edge." This fear can be learned as a child when you are the most vulnerable to negative comments from authority figures. For example, if tears of sadness are responded to with a negative comment or a slap with the back of someone's hand, you will quickly decide feelings are too painful to let out. It is important to acknowledge what it means to feel out of control. Typically, this feeling can create a fear of being weak, helpless, worthless, unprotected, or vulnerable. It is as if you are leaving yourself wide open to be hurt again. This was a lie that was created long ago (unless you are still being hurt this way). This lie was from the hurtful messages that were said or done to you at an earlier time when you were expressing feelings. You must daily remind yourself that you are allowed to identify and express feelings. This is especially true when you fall into the habit of shutting off feelings. Pray to God to reveal the lie and provide guidance to let out your feelings (this process will be discussed in later chapters). To be in control you must allow yourself the ability to step back and consider what is going on inside. Instead of allowing the emotional energy to control you, you have the ability to control the energy by getting it out.

When Ronda cried or became upset as a child, her parents would often yell at her or spank her as a way to stop the crying. This treatment created the belief that something bad or hurtful would happen if she expressed her feelings. As an adult, Ronda could not understand why she was uncomfortable expressing her feelings. Ronda realized her childhood experiences created the lie that feelings were to be feared and the only way to be in control was not to let those feelings out. As Ronda was ready to let go of the lies, she was able to learn how to be free with her feelings.

Do not believe the lies that feelings are something to be feared. You were created with feelings! It was the people around you who took them away. Remember to take control of your feelings before they take control of you. Allowing yourself to feel will empower you to communicate your thoughts and feelings in new and powerful ways. The next chapter will provide the steps to identifying and communicating your feelings.

PS: Words of encouragement

You may have learned for the first time that feelings are normal and you are allowed to express what you feel. This may be hard for you to believe, especially if you have been afraid to feel or told not to feel for most of your life. You don't have to be afraid anymore! Whenever you have feelings stirring inside, tell yourself the truth: "God gave me feelings, and I'm allowed to feel." You may need to tell yourself this over and over again. Do not let what is happening inside keep you controlled by fear. Take control of your feelings! You can do it! "For God did not give us a spirit of timidity, but a spirit of power, of love and of self-discipline" (2 Timothy. 1:7). God knows what you are going through. Pray for help to discover your feelings inside.

The Lord will guide you always; He will satisfy your
needs in a sun-scorched land and will strengthen your
frame. You will be like a well-watered garden,
like a spring whose waters never fail.
(Isaiah. 58:11)

Chapter 8

Steps to finding your feelings

A man finds joy in giving an apt reply — and how
good is a timely word!
(Proverbs 15:23)

Have you ever been in a situation where you became emotionally upset but did not understand why you felt that way? Has someone behaved toward you in a way that was rude, or frustrating, but you did not know what to do with the emotions whirling inside? Do you hold in feelings with periodic emotional outbursts? These are typical responses when you have not learned how to identify and express inner feelings. You can either take control of the feelings or allow the trapped feelings to control you through unhealthy reactions. If you want to release the emotions stirring inside, you must be able to identify your God-given feelings and then give yourself permission to respectfully release them.

When your emotional buttons are pushed

Are there people in your life who make you uncomfortable, scared, or irritated? Are there situations or comments that seem to push you the wrong way? Any time you react with emotions, think of them as your emotional buttons being pushed. The negative emotional buttons are developed from the accumulation of hurtful emotional memories. The more suppressed hurts you have from the past, the more frequent and intense hurtful emotional buttons will be pushed. If you were often hurt as a child from unkind comments, the emotional button of hurt will be pushed in your adulthood if someone makes an unkind comment. However, now that you are an adult, you need to take responsibility for how you react. If someone says an unkind comment, that is only the opinion of that imperfect, rude person. Typically that rude comment is only the trigger to your emotional memories of hurt and shame from rude people in the past. Even though people should not make hurtful comments, you cannot blame that person for your own emotional buttons and you don't need to take the opinion personally. It's only their opinion! This may be a new way to think about taking control of your own life. You may blame others for your reaction so you don't feel any blame or out of control. However, your emotional buttons are often an indication of how you may feel deep inside. If you don't feel good about yourself, the unkind comments will make you defensive as if they were true. As you begin to feel better about yourself by identifying how you feel and uncovering the truth about your shame nature (detailed in later chapters), you will let go of the hurts and the need to blame. As you let go of emotional memories, fewer emotional buttons will be triggered and you will become less defensive when someone makes an unkind comment.

When someone offends you by yelling, criticizing, making hurtful comments, etc., consider them as a source of energy that triggers your emotional buttons of hurt, anger, fear, etc. What you do with that source of emotional energy determines how you react to each situation. People will handle the energy in one of the following ways:

1. If you are like most people, you don't like dealing with the hurtful emotional energy. As I described in the first three chapters, you may feel out of control, afraid, confused, numb, etc. Since you may not know how to feel, you suppress the emotion, pushing the energy deeper inside. You do this with the false belief you are in control of whatever is going on inside. Unfortunately, the emotional energy is still trapped inside, pushing every which way to get out. If you continue to suppress the emotion, the energy will come out in other ways such as angry outbursts, hurtful comments, "I don't care" attitudes, or physical problems such as poor sleep, poor appetite, poor motivation, etc. If you push the emotion deep enough and long enough, you will experience the additional physical and medical problems described in the first two chapters. Since you may not know any other way to feel, you may

continue to live with unhealthy emotions since this feels safe and you have always done it this way. When this happens you are fooled with the belief you are in control. The truth is, you are totally out of control because the energy is controlling you through unhealthy emotions and behaviors.

2. The second and healthier way to deal with the energy is to identify the emotion and let it out. For example, when your emotional buttons are triggered by a harsh comment, the energy from the comment enters your mind and body. To take control of your emotions you must identify the energy and begin to do something with it. This process will allow you to release the energy and reduce other emotional or physical problems that come as a result of holding in the energy. It is extremely important that you identify what you are feeling inside and let it out in a healthy way. To accomplish this, I have developed four questions to help you take control of your feelings. The four questions are important steps to identify the emotional buttons and change from unhealthy patterns of dealing with feelings to healthy ways of expressing feelings.

Instructions: When your emotional buttons are pushed or someone else observes negativity in your behavior, attitude, or mood, ask the following question:

1. **Have someone ask you or ask yourself: WHAT IS GOING ON INSIDE?**
   You may find that identifying unhealthy emotions inside can be a challenge. Often you have developed a comfort zone and have emotionally responded a certain way for most of your life. You may not be aware of your own responses to what is happening around you. Many times you do not recognize that you are having a bad attitude or depressed mood. It will take time to remember to ask yourself this question. It may take the help of someone else and much practice on your part to regularly ask this question, "What is going on inside?" You may want to ask this question whenever a situation triggers your emotional buttons, brings a bad mood, or makes you uncomfortable. Identifying the emotions whirling around inside may be difficult at first. However, as you become sensitive to your own mind and body, and the

more you answer this question, the more you are taking control of your decision to become healthy.

2. **After you have answered the first question and identified that something is wrong, you should have someone ask you or ask yourself: WHAT DO I FEEL INSIDE?**

    (Or, WHAT EMOTIONAL BUTTONS ARE PUSHED?) In order to take control of your feelings, you must identify the emotions that are pushed and whirling inside. Find words to describe those sensations that are going on inside, i.e., hurt, frustration, anxiety, anger, fear, etc. (to help you identify feelings, refer to the chart of faces at the end of this chapter). If you have not learned or have not been allowed to feel throughout your life, this may be the hardest for you. For example, if you grew up in a no feeling no talking about feelings home or an environment where emotions were expressed by yelling, arguing, ridiculing, etc., you will have a difficult time identifying words that describe feelings. Remember you were born with these feelings and you are allowed to feel them. The task of identifying feelings may seem overwhelming at first, but the more you express yourself, the easier it becomes. The hardest part may be giving yourself permission to feel. When you are asked this question, you need to play the role of a detective and find the feelings inside. When you identify the feelings or what emotional button was pushed, allow yourself to release these feelings by saying or writing down "I feel" statements, i.e., "I feel . . hurt, angry, frustrated, scared," etc. Remember that suppressed feelings are like unhealthy emotional energy that will fester and come out in unhealthy emotions and behaviors. For the unhealthy energy to be released, you must GET IT OUT through telling someone, writing it, or praying it out loud, using "I feel..." statements.

What should I do if I cannot feel anything?

If you lived or currently live in a home with unhealthy relationships, you may have blocked out or become numb to your feelings. Your feelings have been pushed down so deep you may be afraid to let them out or not know how to let them out. Do not give up trying to identify your feelings! Remember, God gave you those feelings and you are allowed to use them. You need to decide to change what you learned in the past and take control of your feelings instead of letting them take control of you. When you cannot feel anything, you need a trusted family member or friend to listen and watch your reactions to help identify what is happening inside of you. If you still do not know what to feel after looking at the sheet of emotional faces, identify how your body is physically reacting. Do you have a stomachache, headache, pounding of your heart, tightness in your chest, or any ache in your body? When you identify those aches and pains, describe to someone what your body feels like and how those aches and pains make you feel. Be a detective and search for what your body is telling you.

For example, if your husband yelled and you suddenly decided to go to your bedroom to get away, you should look at the four questions. Since your reaction was to get away, you realize that something is wrong—which answers question number one. However, you get stuck on question number two, because you have no idea how you feel. Start playing detective to find how your body is reacting. You have tightness in the chest and nervousness throughout your body. As a detective, you figure that must mean you're scared. That's it, you're scared! If you have a difficult time playing detective on your own, ask someone to help you discover what is going on inside. The more you answer these questions, the easier it will become.

3. **After you have answered the second question and identified what you feel, you should have someone ask you or ask yourself: WHY DO I FEEL THIS WAY INSIDE?**

Think back over the past one to eight hours to determine what circumstances may have taken place that would have triggered these feelings. Often daily events can be triggers for emotional memories you have continually put off wanting to deal with. You may suppress the hurt until an event hours later triggers the emotional memory of the hurt or in some situations your mind dredges up disturbing thoughts and feelings when you begin to relax. For example, when you cannot sleep because your mind is whirling around with troubling thoughts, use these four questions to get rid of what is bothering you. You should say out loud or write down the answer to this question through statements such as, "I feel angry because...." Once you discover why you feel that way you do, you have the option to go on to the next question.

4. **After you have answered the third question and identified why you feel that way, you have the option to answer this fourth question. WHAT WILL I DO ABOUT THESE FEELINGS?**

This question is a suggestion to primarily help you find constructive ways to deal with the original issues that may be causing the feelings.

For example, it is important that you deal with your problem by continuing to talk out loud, pray out loud, or write down your feelings. This will allow proper release of the emotional energy that has been festering from the original problem. To help, you may want to say or write out your thoughts about the following:

Who was involved? What happened to make me feel this way? When did I start feeling this way? How long have I been feeling this way? What can I say or do to change what happened?

As you answer these questions and let go of the unhealthy emotional energy, you will be able to feel calmer and think more clearly. As a result, you may discover information that will enable you to feel more in control by understanding the problem better and beginning to take some action. Maybe the action will be as simple as talking to someone, writing a letter, or going as far as respectfully confronting the offender. Sometimes the circumstances will not allow you to verbally take action against a person or problem. So you may say, "Why bother talking about it? That will not change what happened." You are correct; you may not be able to change the original problem. However, it is important to do something with the negative emotional energy created by the problem before the negative energy destroys you. Even if you were a victim of something that you feel helpless to change, you do not need to let the suppressed feelings fool you into becoming a helpless victim. If you do nothing about what happened, the end result will be repeated triggers of emotions with feelings of anger, anxiety, panic, mood swings, helplessness, etc. If time passes without a release of the negative emotional energy, the trapped feelings will turn into bitterness, resentment, and depression. By doing nothing about the situation, the emotion will control you, keeping you in bondage to the belief that you are a helpless victim to the situation. By making a decision to do something for yourself, you are taking action that gives an emotional release and control over your own life.

Changing undesirable behavior

You read in earlier chapters that suppressed feelings can lead to undesirable behaviors such as unexplained anxiety, fear, panic, anger outbursts, etc. The first step to changing undesirable behavior is to first identify what you are feeling and release that feeling either at the time the emotional buttons are triggered or as soon as possible. To help you break those patterns of behavior, it is advisable to have a spouse, family member and/or trusted friend(s) become your accountability partner(s) by asking the questions in this chapter. Everyone in your family should participate in using these questions, since the more people there are around you talking about feelings, the faster you will succeed in making changes.

To allow the questions to work, you may want to give family or close friends permission to ask you these questions. Tell each person: "I give you permission to ask me these questions." For you to share feelings with others, you may want to get their permission for you to tell them your feelings. Ask each person: "Do you give me permission to say how I feel and why I feel that way?" As you give people permission to work with you through these four questions, you must be honest and respectful with your answers. The accountability partner(s) must be willing to allow you to be honest and release what you feel inside. If you are alone, go through the exercise by writing the answers in a journal or say them out loud through prayer or talking to yourself. It does not matter which way you decide to release the feelings. However, in order for the release of feelings to properly take place you must get the feelings out by verbalizing or writing the answers to the four questions. As you begin to regularly release the feelings inside, you will break free from old patterns and begin to feel the peace of mind that God originally intended.

Bill's story

When Bill came to see me he was experiencing daily feelings of anger and anxiety with mood swings. For many years he would also have symptoms of anxiety attacks that were triggered by confrontations with family or coworkers. He admitted not knowing what to do with these overwhelming feelings that often came from the accumulation of job and family problems. The only way to survive, he thought, was not to express his feelings at all. Bill would handle daily problems at home and work by either walking away or saying nothing. This would continue until some small issue would cause an outburst of anger. When there was confrontation with someone, Bill was aware that inner emotions were stirred up, but he never knew what to do with them. Over the years Bill believed not having feelings was the normal and acceptable way to respond. Bill recalled that as a child, his parents did not show many feelings and he was discouraged toward expressing his own feelings. Consequently, Bill assumed that if he expressed feelings his parents would disapprove of him.

As an adult, Bill realized the many years of holding in feelings were creating a buildup of negative energy, like an expanding balloon ready to pop. As a temporary release, his body was letting out the negative energy through anger, anxiety, mood swings, and physical problems that were slowly destroying him emotionally and physically. The only way he knew to deal with conflicts was to walk away or shut down emotionally. He was conditioned to believe expressing feelings was wrong and no amount of explanation from friends was able to convince him otherwise. He intellectually understood that he should not respond the way he did, but emotionally he was held captive to some underlying fear that something might happen if he actually expressed himself. He did not know what to do and he was afraid deep inside to let out his feelings.

In counseling Bill realized he continued the same unhealthy responses as an adult that he learned in his childhood years. He also realized his deep-rooted unhealthy behaviors would not change unless he received help from others. Bill learned about the four questions and asked his wife to help him be accountable them. Bill wrote the questions on paper to have available in his car, office, and home. He gave a copy of the questions to his wife and children during a family meeting and discussed how to ask the questions. To help Bill, everyone in the family agreed to participate by giving each other permission to ask the questions to one another. Since this was new to the family, Bill encouraged everyone to be patient for the first few weeks. When something pushed his emotional buttons at work, Bill would either write down the answer to the four questions or call his wife to say the answers over the phone. Driving home from work Bill would think about what upset him during the day and talk out loud the answers to the questions as he drove. Bill found it helpful for his wife and children to ask him the questions when they saw a negative reaction. The children began to find these steps fun and enjoyed the extra attention they were getting. Bill admitted it was not easy at first to identify and express feelings, but each time he expressed them, it became easier. Using the four questions, Bill learned to identify what was triggering his emotions and how to express feelings to let go of the emotional stresses and physical symptoms that plagued him for years. The questions also reduced his repression of feelings and reduced the need for emotional outbursts and out of control feelings.

Like Bill, you may not know how to identify and properly express your feelings. Do your emotional buttons get pushed often or do you have the habit of holding in feelings and letting the unhealthy feelings control you? Whatever happens, you need to take responsibility for the feelings you have inside. If you do not take responsibility and change how you identify and express feelings, you will pass the same old pattern on to the next generation. Now that you have a way to change this pattern, you have no excuse. You have the opportunity and responsibility to change a way of expressing yourself that may have gone on for generations before you. It is an honor for you to discover an unhealthy pattern of your life and be the specific person to make a healthy change for all the generations to come. Starting today, you can change how you feel for the rest of your life by asking the following four questions. Write the questions down on little card so you can take them wherever you go. These questions will change your life. What is going on inside? What do I feel inside? Why do I feel this way inside? What will I do about these feelings?

PS: Words of encouragement:

You have probably learned something that you have not known before. You may think that identifying and expressing your feelings will be a difficult task. You may not know how to feel and wonder if you can do this. You may even be scared just thinking about saying your feelings. Remember that God gave you feelings and it is natural to feel. It was people that made you fear the feelings that you have. God is honored when you express the feelings that He gave you. You do not need to be ashamed, feel guilty, or run away from these feelings. The only way you will feel free is to express your feelings and let go of the hurtful emotional memories. This will be one of the most rewarding things that you accomplish for yourself and the people in your life. The effort you put into releasing your feelings will be one of the most powerful things you can do for yourself. Becoming healthier and wiser will be your reward.

What are you feeling inside?

Chapter 9

Discovering and overcoming how your past influenced you

'For I know the plans I have for you,' declares
the LORD, 'plans to prosper you and not to harm
you, plans to give you hope and a future'.
(Jeremiah 29:11)

You have already learned in Chapter Two how the past greatly influenced your life. You started out as a trusting child, open to whatever the caregivers brought your way, whether it was words of encouragement with loving arms or destructive words with hurtful hands. At that young age the experiences stirred up fear, tears, laughter, or whatever type of physical or emotional response the circumstances would trigger. God intended your responses to be an automatic natural reflex, like taking your next breath. The caregiver's response was a critical influence in determining how you physically and emotionally expressed yourself and how you handled life's ups and downs later in life.

Once you get a glimpse of your past behaviors and feelings, you will unlock the door to change how you currently think, feel, and behave. You may be thinking, "Why should I dredge up the past? The past is over and I want to move on with my life." My answer to that is, "You are already dredging up the past because you're living in it!" The reason why you are struggling with unhealthy feelings, destructive behaviors, shame nature, self-judgment, and other emotional or physical issues is because they are all extensions from the past. Your current unhealthy feelings are the result of unhealed hurts from the past you continue to avoid. I am not going to drag you through the past but help you learn to understand it. I will not be dragging you through the pain and misery of the past because you are probably living it every day, and do not know it! You will not know how to change how you feel or effectively pray to God for help until you know what to ask for. You will not be able to change the way you think and feel until you understand the reasons you are reacting that way.

How you felt as a child

Take some time to think about your childhood. Picture your home or the place you spent the most time. Was it a comfortable place to live or a place where you felt a lot of stress or hurt or felt nothing? Picture in your mind the way you related to your mother and father or the other caregivers who were involved with you. Did they make you feel special about yourself or did you receive a lot of criticism? You may not want to remember what happened; you may not remember anything, or you may have a mixture of good and bad memories. Whatever memories come to mind, chances are you did not deal with many of the feelings that came your way. Those hurtful, ugly, feelings continue to stir around inside, keeping you in the past without your even knowing it. Lets begin to unlock the past in order that you may understand it and know how to more effectively get rid of it.

Instructions: Take some time to think about your childhood years (preferably between age four years and thirteen years old). If your early memories are vague, take time to think about that time of your life before you complete is section (if you need to, include the years of age ten through fifteen). Looking at the statements found in both columns, circle the statement that most appropriately fits you during that time of childhood.

AS A CHILD, I WAS:		I WAS:
1. Usually not allowed to express feelings (tears, anger).	or	1. Usually allowed to express my feelings (tears, anger).

2. Not able to talk easily   or   2. Able to talk easily about my
   about my personal life.   personal life.

3. Not emotionally close to   or   3. Emotionally close to mother
   mother (few or no hugs &   (many hugs & kisses).
   kisses).

4. Not emotionally close to   or   4. Emotionally close to father
   father (few or no hugs &   (many hugs & kisses).
   kisses).

5. Not feeling good about   or   5. Feeling good about myself.
   myself.

6. Sad more than I was happy. or   6. Happy more than I was sad.

7. Not feeling very safe or   or   7. Feeling very safe and secure at
   secure at home.   home.

8. Always wondering if   or   8. Not wondering if something bad
   something bad was going   was going to happen at home.
   to happen at home.

9. Received more criticism   or   9. Received more praise than
   than praise from caregivers.   criticism from caregivers.

10. Feeling like I was never   or   10. Felt like I could do most
    able to do anything right.   anything right.

11. Not comforted very much   or   11. Comforted most of the time
    when I felt hurt.   when I felt hurt.

12. My caregivers often argued or   12. My caregivers did not argue and
    or yelled which made me   yell very much.
    very uncomfortable.

When you are done, take a few minutes break from reading before you continue with the next set of statements.

119

How you feel as an adult

Think about your life now. Think about the years after you left home and what it was like to be away from your family. Picture in your mind the relationships you have now and how you interact in them. Most importantly, think about yourself and how you have felt inside through the last five years. Have you felt good about yourself and your accomplishments? How are you with establishing emotionally close relationships? How are you with expressing your thoughts and feelings? These are the thoughts that will help you understand yourself as an adult. This is not a test to judge you or a way to find "right" or "wrong" answers. Instead, this is a way to paint a picture of your life right now. Lets begin to understand you as an adult.

Instructions: Take some time to think about the last five or more years. Looking at the statements found in both columns; circle the statement that most appropriately fits you during this time.

AS AN ADULT, I AM:

1. Usually not able to express my feelings (i.e., tears).

2. Not able to talk to others about personal problems.

3. Difficult to become emotionally close to other adults.

4. Not comfortable when I receive praise or compliments.

5. Not feeling very good about myself.

6. More sad than I am happy.

I AM:

1. Usually able to express my feelings (i.e., tears).

2. Able to talk to others about personal problems.

3. Able to become emotionally close to other adults.

4. Comfortable when I receive praise or compliments.

5. Feeling good about myself.

6. More happy than I am sad.

(each joined by "or")

7. Not feeling safe and secure   or   7. Feeling very safe and secure
   with new situations.   with new life situations.

8. Always wondering if   or   8. Not always wondering if
   something bad will happen.   something bad will happen.

9. Feeling like I can never   or   9. Feeling like I can do most
   do anything right.   anything right.

10. Not comfortable when I   or   10. Comforted when I receive
    receive sympathy.   sympathy.

11. When someone argues or   or   11. When someone argues around
    yells at me I become   me I do not become
    uncomfortable.   uncomfortable.

Final instructions:

1. Now that you are done with both lists, look over the adult list and read the circled answers.
2. After reading the adult answers, look over the childhood list and read the circled answers.
3. Compare the list of adult circled answers with the list of childhood circled answers.

If you are like many of the people I meet, you circled similar answers on both lists. As you reviewed both lists, you may have seen the similarities and differences of what happened in your childhood compared with what you are like as an adult. Do you allow yourself to express feelings any differently now compared to your childhood? Is it still difficult to develop relationships or become emotionally close to people? Do you currently think about yourself or life like you did as a child? Do you accept comfort or praise from others any differently than you did as a child? Are you able to deal with conflict or angry people any differently as an adult than you did as a child? If many of the answers circled are similar, chances are you have continued what was learned from childhood. If the child and adult answers are totally opposite, either you are fortunate enough to resolve your childhood issues or you are blocking many of the past memories. The past will always have an impact on the present. Let's begin to understand your answers.

What happened in childhood

It is important to remember from Chapter Two that throughout childhood (particularly before age eight or nine), you naturally responded to situations by feeling emotions inside. When something hurtful happened, your young, innocent mind reacted by simply feeling hurt. You were too young to sort out, rationalize, or analyze why you were experiencing the feelings inside. All you experienced was an uncomfortable sensation that became an emotional memory. For example, if your caregiver yelled at you for an unknown reason, you would experience a whirling of hurt inside. Since you had not developed the ability to rationalize why it happened, you would automatically feel hurt and believe you did something wrong. As you read in earlier chapters, your childhood actions and words were often an extension of what you felt and believed. If your caregivers regularly criticized your thoughts and actions, you would create the belief your actions and words were wrong. The caregiver's hurtful words and how you reacted would be stored in emotional memories that would be transferred into adulthood. As a result, these emotional memories would continue into adulthood with all the avoidance behaviors, suppressed hurts, and unhealthy beliefs that were learned in childhood.

As a child, picture your bowl of cereal that accidentally spilled in the living room with your caregiver becoming angry and yelling at the top of their lungs. All you felt were these big ugly sensations swirling inside like a tornado. You wanted to run away from these awful feelings, but you felt physically trapped with a big emotional ache in your chest. Maybe you ran to your room or you were told to go there. You may have fallen onto your bed, sobbing in a massive heap of hurt and despair, believing you were the worst person in the world. "I'm such a terrible person! How could I do such a bad thing?" you would tell yourself. You did not want to have this awful feeling inside, so you locked it away in your emotional memory bank hoping it would never come out again. You did not know these feelings of fear, sadness, hurt, and guilt were normal reactions. You only learned that feelings were confusing, scary, ugly, wrong, and something you wanted to lock away.

What happens as an adult?

Now think of your adult years. What happens when you are confronted with someone who disappoints you, becomes upset, or speaks unkind words? Are your emotional buttons pushed with uncomfortable feelings or nervousness in your stomach like a churning washing machine? Do the emotional buttons trigger a trapped and scared feeling, wanting to get away from the situation before something bad happens? Maybe you feel nothing or a numb feeling all over. Chances are, your adult events are triggering childhood emotional memories that have been transferred into the adult years. When your spouse yells and you want to shrivel up and hide, the emotional button of hurt triggers an emotional memory of when someone criticized you as a child. That is why it is so confusing when dealing with adult situations and you may not feel like you are handling the situation in an adult manner (or be told you are not acting like an adult).

You are living in an adult body, experiencing adult situations that trigger feelings created in childhood. You have experienced the feelings for so long, you do not recognize their childhood origin. The next time something negative happens to you, you will naturally have a reaction of dislike. However, the majority of the feelings are from your past. The adult situation was only the trigger, while the childhood emotional memory was the origin of the adult emotional reaction. For example, when your spouse yells at you, the adult part of you may not like the yelling and should respectfully tell your spouse you did not appreciate it. However, if you become overwhelmingly upset, shut down emotionally, or have some other emotional reaction that does not seem to fit, chances are you are dredging up reactions from your emotional memories. This reaction is what I call childlikeness.

Childlikeness reactions in an adult body

Through the years, you grew up biologically, maturing into an adult body with all the problems and responsibilities that go with it. Even though your body biologically matured from a child to an adult, your feelings might not have matured at the same rate. When repeated childhood hurts and traumas were not allowed to heal and were suppressed into emotional memories, it would be like living with an open festering emotional wound that does not heal. As this open wound transfers into adulthood, you would continue similar childlike reactions whenever someone triggered the emotional memories of that childhood emotional wound. Childlikeness is when your thoughts, feelings, and behaviors tend to resemble a child's level of emotional reaction rather than the emotional response of an adult. This makes it more difficult to overcome issues of shame, self-judgment, destructive messages, and inner struggles of hurts and unforgiveness. Childlikeness contributes to the reasons why your emotional buttons get pushed so easily; why you may not be able to maintain healthy relationships (even with God); or why you have difficulty moving on with issues in life. When stressful events happen in adulthood, your emotional buttons trigger the childhood emotional memories to react much the same way you did as a child. You cannot seem to do anything differently because you did not learn a new way of responding. Your emotional memories are still festering inside and your emotional buttons trigger the feelings to come out with the childlikeness reactions. When Sam became frustrated during arguments with his wife he would use put-down statements toward his wife as if to get in the last word. He would stomp his feet as he left the room and slam doors on his way out of the house. Sam would become easily defensive and not talk to his wife for several days after an argument. When the wife talked to Sam's mother it was revealed he would often get his way as a child and temper tantrums were a frequent occurrence. Finally his wife's eyes were open to seeing Sam's behavior as a childlike temper tantrum in an adult body.

At first, childlikeness reactions will be hard for you to notice because that is the only way you may know how to act. Childlikeness reactions are those reactions learned as a child that are observed in adulthood when situations trigger your emotional buttons. The following are some examples of childlikeness reactions:

- **Adult temper tantrums**. Exhibiting childlikeness behaviors in an adult body, when circumstances do not go your way. For example, whining, stomping your feet, pouting, sulking, moodiness, slamming doors, crying, yelling for little reason, or other tantrum-like reactions.
- **Avoidance behaviors**. Behaviors used to hide, escape, or get away from situations that are not physically threatening. For example, fantasies, day dreaming, walking away (or wanting to walk away) during a conversation, staying in bed for no reason, going out of your way to avoid someone or something, not speaking to someone, holding grudges, silent treatments.

- **Avoiding feelings**. When you avoid inner feelings and do not allow yourself to respectfully express your own thoughts and feelings. For example, not saying how you think or feel when you are offended; not expressing your inner opinions, needs, or desires; emotionally shutting down when something hurtful happens; being afraid something will happen if you express your feelings; not being able to find words, as if your mind freezes or becomes numb, blank, or confused.
- **Self-centeredness**. This is when the world must focus around you (it is usually easier for someone else to observe this in you), for example, when you expect your needs, wants, and desires to come first with little consideration of the feelings, needs, and desires of others. In addition, you frequently become jealous, controlling, or demanding toward others.

Now that you have realized more about your past, do you want to change? It is my hope you would give me a resounding "Yes!" To begin the process of changing the childlikeness, you need to allow the emotional part of the child that is hurt to heal and allow the emotional energy to come out through expressions of emotion. Most of all, you need to learn that you are allowed to have feelings and are good enough to allow those feelings to come out. Let's begin to put together what we have learned so far about your past and the importance of feeling those hurts.

You learned by example

As a child, when you fell and hurt yourself, were you able to seek love and comfort from your caregivers when you needed them? Did your caregivers allow you to freely express feelings when you were hurt? Did you feel safe in going to your caregivers for comfort and receive caring words or loving kisses for comfort? Did you feel secure and comfortable in returning to your caregivers anytime for more comfort? If you answered mostly "No" to these questions, then you were not emotionally parented. You did not receive the reassurance that someone was available for you when you really needed it. You may not have felt safe to be yourself and freely express what feelings were in your heart and mind. When you did not receive love and comfort from caregivers, you did not have an example from whom to learn how to feel secure, how to trust, love and comfort yourself , or how to allow others to love and comfort you.

You should consider the childhood years like one long period of learning how to survive the ups and downs of life. You should also consider your caregivers as the role models with their words, actions, and beliefs as your examples. If you did not have other examples to compare with, you would not know there were different ways to think, behave, and feel. That is a big reason why you stay in your comfort zone of childlikeness reactions, even when your behavior does not make sense. Often the childlikeness reactions were created from hurtful situations where you did not learn the steps necessary as to what to do with that hurt. You must begin to eliminate the past hurts and learn how to comfort, love, and express yourself. Consequently, your childlikeness gets in the way of handling the daily ups and downs and does not allow proper healing of the hurts that may continue to come out when emotional buttons are pushed.

For example, picture a young child named Johnny, who walks in the front door crying from a bicycle accident. The ideal emotional parenting for the child would look something like this: The father says to the child, "Johnny come over here and sit on my lap." The father carefully wipes Johnny's eyes while putting his arms around Johnny. The father says, "You look hurt. Tell me what's wrong." Johnny sobs and whimpers as he shows the little scrapes on his hands and tells his father what happened. The father replies to what Johnny says, "That sounds awful to have that happen. You must have been really hurt. Let me kiss your hands to make them better." The father kisses Johnny's hands and rubs his back. Johnny's face immediately begins to brighten up. "Are you feeling better now?" asked the father. Johnny says, "Yes," as the father gives him a hug. Johnny says he wants to go back to playing outside. The fathers says, "Go ahead and play. Be careful next time." Johnny goes on his merry way as if little happened.

Although this may not happen for all hurts, the scenario gives the general picture of what any child needs to receive with their hurt. Even though the hurt was minor from an adult point of view, the hurt was traumatic in the little world of that child. Similar to Johnny, the treatment by your caregiver was the training ground by which you will deal with the ups and downs of hurts as an adult. The essence of what Johnny experienced was identifying the hurt; expressing the hurt; comforting the hurt; letting go of the hurt; and knowing what to do when the hurt comes again. Johnny was validated as a person and made to feel important because his feelings were important. He felt comfortable in expressing his needs because he felt safe and was allowed to express his feelings. He felt loved and comforted because of the kisses, the warm arms around him, and the kind words. He felt safe enough to express himself because the caregiver allowed freedom to feel and allowed him to behave as a child when he was hurt. He was able to bounce back to happiness quickly because he was able to let go of the hurt and he had the reassurance that the caregiver was available for any hurt in the future. Johnny felt secure in his world because no matter what happened, he had the reassurance of being comforted. That feeling of safety, security, comfort, reassurance, and freedom to feel was carried into his adult life. He had a greater ability to handle life's ups and downs because of the emotional foundation he received to handle those ups and downs as a child.

If the type of comfort Johnny received is foreign to you, chances are you have a tendency to be stuck in a childlikeness where you may have: difficulty expressing your feelings; difficulty letting go of hurts; not feeling comforted; and feeling insecure or unloved. You continue to search for relationships to fulfill the unmet needs of love and security which were unavailable from your caregivers. Unfortunately, the disappointment continues because of the emotionally unavailable people you continue to let into your life. You have difficulty finding the love you need, but have not learned how to accept the love when it is freely given to you. If you received little comfort from your caregivers, chances are you were forced to become emotionally strong and independent to survive the hurts in your life. The fact that you have become strong is an asset and credit to your survival. Unfortunately, your need to be strong and in control can hinder your ability to let others into your life or allow you to be comforted, loved, and have the ability to let go of hurts.

Like Johnny, you have a right to receive all the love and comfort that is available. However, you will not be able to receive any love and change emotionally, as long as you are stuck in the childlikeness state of mind and heart. You need to begin recognizing the difference between the thoughts, feelings, and behaviors of childlikeness and those of the adult.

Separating the adult from the childlikeness

In order for the adult part of you to help the child part, you need to realize there is a difference and learn to separate them. You may have been using the same childlike thoughts, feelings, and behaviors for so long that you are convinced they are normal. Even if you realized through this book that you have childlikeness reactions and think destructive thoughts, you will not change unless you learn another way to respectfully treat yourself. The emotional responses you created in childhood may have become so locked into your life that you do not realize there are other ways to react. Whenever you have childlikeness reaction, you may feel trapped and helpless to change. Those are the old lies of destructive feelings and thoughts that you have built your life around. As you stop using childlikeness reactions, you will find the truth. You need to recognize when you have childlikeness reactions and separate them out from what you would feel, think, or say as an adult. You may say, "But I don't know how to react as an adult!" You do know how to react, but you do not realize it. Use this example to help you understand how you can react as an adult:

If you were at a large department store and a scared little child who was crying came to you, saying, "I can't find my Mommy, I can't find my Mommy. I don't know what to do," what would you say or do to help that child? Would you helplessly fall on the floor, sitting in a daze, afraid to say anything? Would you start crying and shouting right along with the child? Would you become upset, saying to her, "Go away! go away! Your crying makes me scared. I don't know what to do with you!" Chances are you would not react that way. Those behaviors would be acting just like the child. The helpless, crying, scared child that came to you in the store was a lost victim of circumstance with no threat to you. As an adult you would probably bend down to her level and in a caring way tell her, "You seem to be lost. Try not to worry, I will help you find your mother." You would comfort her by taking her hand and leading her to some safe place. You would find direction and guidance through people in the store that could get her the help she needed. You would probably need to reassure the little girl over and over again that she was going to be all right. After it was all done, you would feel pretty good inside for helping the child become safe.

If you could help that little child, you can certainly help the helpless, scared, childlike emotions that are stuck inside you. If your emotional buttons are pushed, remember, the emotions are not a real physical threat; they only feel like a threat. The feeling of a threat comes from the frightening and hurtful childhood experiences that were transferred into adulthood. When helpless emotional buttons are pushed, you need to tell yourself it will be all right, as if you are comforting a child with nurturing words, letting a child know that you are in charge and will take care of the problem. You may say, "I am safe now. I can take care of the problem." If you experienced extremely traumatic childhood hurts, focusing on inner feelings may trigger overwhelming childlikeness reactions that bring confusion or make your mind go blank. Until you become more familiar with the techniques in this book to change those reactions, the following may be helpful during extreme childlikeness reactions where you mentally shut down. You may want to focus on an object you use as an adult (i.e., an adult picture of you, car keys, driver's license, kitchen object, etc.) to bring you back to the adult part of you. Repeat to yourself or pray out loud statements such as, "I am physically an adult," "I am safe (or, I am safe with Jesus)," "I don't need to be afraid (or, Jesus take my fear and give me peace of mind)."

Finding the adult feelings

If you grew up in a home where you did not receive much emotional parenting as described above, you would not know how to comfort yourself when you are hurt. This does not mean you are immature; this means you carried into your adulthood all that you learned from childhood. You cannot be at fault for that. However, now that you know what happened, it is up to you to make the changes. The childlikeness has been so common in your life it has become difficult to recognize between childlikeness and adult thoughts, behaviors, and feelings. For example, if someone makes a nasty comment at you, your emotional buttons will be pushed. However, how you feel inside and how you react with behaviors can mean the difference between childlikeness and adult reactions. If your buttons trigger a reaction of pure emotional defensiveness, you are reacting from your childlikeness. If you react with some emotion that comes out with rational, behavior and logical statements about what you feel and think, that is adult.

To help you determine whether your response is coming from childlikeness or adult reactions, the following steps will be helpful.

1. **Identify your feelings.** The best way to discern what is going on in your heart and mind is to determine how you feel. As you go through these questions, it would be helpful to say the answers out loud or write them down to get the negative energy out. First identify what

you feel inside using the following three questions (detailed in the chapter, Steps to Finding Your Feelings):
- What is going on inside of me?
- What do I feel right now?
- Why do I feel this way inside?

2. After you identify the feelings inside, you may want to uncover whether you are responding with childlikeness or adult reactions. You can use these simple questions anywhere and any time you want to uncover whether you need to feel or react the way you do. Since it may start out becoming difficult to answer these questions from an objective viewpoint, it may be helpful to have someone work with you on the answers. Even if you do not have help from others, you should quickly master these questions over time. After you identify the feelings inside, ask the following questions:
- **Is there anything that I have done wrong that caused me to feel this way?**

In most situations you will discover there is nothing you have done to cause the problem. Your emotional buttons of guilt, anxiety, hurt, fear, etc., have been triggered for so long, you created the belief that you were supposed to feel that way.
- **Am I responding with a childlike response or adult-like response?**

If the response is primarily a me-centered reaction, with a lot of negative emotions and behaviors, it tends to be childlikeness. If the response comes from logical thinking with rational behaviors, it tends to be an adult reaction. (Chapter Eleven describes me-centered and logical reactions in more detail.)
- **Do I need to feel this way?**

Does the type and intensity of emotions and behaviors that come out of you really help the situation? Do the emotional buttons trigger childlikeness unhealthy reactions? You may want to have someone help you determine if you really need to continue reacting the way you do.
- **How can I respond differently as an adult?**

Think of alternative ways you should behave and feel as an adult. You may want to have someone help you with this question. (The chapters ahead will help answer this question.)

3. Receive comfort and repeated reassurance. Care for yourself by allowing God and others to help you. Asking for help does not mean you are weak or out of control. When you ask for help you are saying, "I

am taking control of my situation and finding the best way to handle it." The same negative feelings have been triggered for so long, you may never have realized there was another way to feel. If you become overwhelmed and need reassurance, you may want to tell yourself statements such as:

- I am safe (or, Jesus keep me safe).
- I can take care of myself (or, Jesus will take care for me).
- I don't have to feel this way (or, Jesus take away this feeling).
- I don't need to be afraid (or, Jesus take my fear and bring me peace of mind).

You may have a difficult time allowing others into your personal world. Allow a friend, family member, or God to come into your life to let their comfort, guidance, and friendship help you. If a loved one or friend needed personal time to talk about a hurting issue you would probably take time to help them. So, why not ask God to bring someone into your life to help you?

4. Give it away. Whether you talk about the hurt, write it out in a journal, or pray it out to God, you must literally get it out of your mind and heart. God wants you to give Him your hurts and burdens to bring healing and reduce the daily burdens. "Come to Me, all you who are weary and burdened, and I will give you rest. Take My yoke upon you, and learn from Me, for I am gentle and humble in heart, and you will find rest for your souls" (Matthew 11:28,29).

5. Think of your past experiences. When you do not feel good about yourself, often you will not feel good about your accomplishments or feel comfortable trying something new. When you were in a difficult situation in the past, did you make it through? Chances are you were able to survive that past experience. Although you may have endured a painful past, those experiences will provide the wisdom and direction for the difficulties yet to come.

Building a firm foundation

Emotional buttons that trigger childlikeness reactions can cause confusion and distort your ability to think, feel, and behave as a mature adult. If you logically think of the emotional needs of a child, you realize there is a great need for being safe and feeling loved. If you did not receive very much unconditional love, you did not know what you were missing. When you are loved as a child, you should have received physical touch and emotional messages that would create in your heart and mind messages such as, "I am important and what I say and feel is important," "I am good enough to be loved," "I can make mistakes and still be good enough," "I am good enough no matter what happens," "God loves me just the way I am." These messages would create a secure belief in yourself, which would strengthen your ability to battle life's ups and downs. Not receiving a secure foundation of love and acceptance as a child would be similar to using a sand foundation for a house. When the hardships of life came your way, such as windy arguments, rainy days of depression, and storms of criticism, the weak foundation made it a struggle to fight those battles of life. Many times it seems easier just to give up. To make matters worse, the messages you received in the past (or currently) may have created the belief that you were not good enough to receive love and acceptance. As a result, the weak belief in yourself often made it harder to muster the courage to stand up for yourself or step out in faith to make your life better.

The insecure foundation continues the same destructive childhood cycle of lies that you cannot do anything right and you are not good enough to try. Without a firm foundation to believe in yourself, your daily struggles with self-destructive thinking and behaviors will seem like living life is one battle after another. Like a strong and secure concrete foundation of a house, a secure belief that you are good enough is necessary to withstand the hurts that life throws your way. Although the concrete foundation may crack or shift during the storms of life, the knowledge that you are good enough, no matter what you do, will help you be secure to react more with logic and appropriate emotion, rather than feeling out of control and child-likeness emotion. Whether it is a building structure, personality, or relationship, you need a strong foundation to stand the test of time. To stand strong and tall throughout your life, you need to build a sturdy foundation with healthy beliefs, thoughts, words, and actions. The following will be helpful to build a healthy foundation in your life:

- Stand on a solid rock, not on sinking sand: Do not let the hurtful messages of the past create a sandy foundation that makes you struggle to believe in yourself and struggle with finding meaning in life. You must radically change the old negative thinking by standing on a solid foundation of truth. Even with the disappointments, hurts, and lies of life you can stand on the everlasting true words of Jesus Christ found in the New Testament. "Therefore everyone who hears these words of mine and puts them into practice is like a wise man who built his house on the rock" (Matthew 7:24). Use the techniques in this book to identify what emotional buttons are being triggered, release those feelings, and discover if those feelings are the truth.

- Find positive people with positive attitudes: The significant people in your life (past and present) will influence your heart, mind, and soul. You will become just like the people and places you are with the most. Find activities that are positive and find a Christ-centered church that cares about you, with activities for you and your family. You need to fellowship with positive-thinking people and stay away from those who give out negative and critical comments. If you must live or work with people that are critical, care for yourself by allowing God, a Christian professional, and others with positive attitudes to help you. Asking for help does not mean you are weak or out of control. When you ask for help you are saying, "I am taking control of my situation and finding the best way to handle it."

- Fill your body with healthy things: When you put unhealthy food in your body, your body will physically feel unhealthy. You must eat and drink healthy to feel healthy. Stay away from foods that affect your body in ways you find yourself overindulging (alcohol, over the counter drugs, caffeine, excessive sugar). For example, stay away from food with excessive sugar, since it can contribute to depression, anxiety, and deplete the vital nutrients in your body, which increases overall poor health. Eat three meals a day with proper nutritional value for your body to have the right amount of fuel to burn. Drink plenty of water (rather than coffee or soda pop – which increases sugar intake and dehydrates your body). For further information you may want to talk with a health care professional about your general nutrition.

- Fill your mind with healthy things: When you put unhealthy thoughts in your mind, you will think and struggle with those unhealthy thoughts. Negative thoughts will make you a negative person. Challenge yourself to find the positive in your daily situations. Stay away from videos, television shows, magazines, music, people, etc. that affect your mind in negative ways. Fill your mind with things that are pleasing. "Finally, brothers, whatever is true, whatever is noble, whatever is

133

right, whatever is pure, whatever is lovely, whatever is admirable – if anything is excellent or praiseworthy – think about such things. Whatever you have learned or received or heard from me, or seen in me – put it into practice. And the God of peace will be with you" (Philippians 4:8, 9). Read encouraging literature (especially the New Testament Bible), listen to uplifting music, and fill your eyes with only uplifting sights. Every day tell yourself positive statements that have encouraging messages. Your heart, mind, and soul need to be healed through repeating positive, uplifting, affirming words. Write encouraging Bible scriptures on paper to carry with you or place around your home or office. Or write the following list down on small cards and place the cards around your house and place of work. Say these positive statements in the morning and at night.

- I am good enough.
- I am precious in God's sight.
- I am made in God's image.
- God forgives me.
- I am a unique and wonderful person.
- I am free to express the feelings that God gave me.
- I do not need to listen to and believe the destructive messages I hear.
- I can accept the good things that God has for me today.

Now that you are aware of your past, there is no reason why you need to continue the same thoughts, feelings, and behaviors that originated in the past. You now can begin taking control to make the changes you have always wanted. Most importantly, you must seek help from others if you expect to be successful in making these changes. If you do not accept help, you will have a difficult time trying to change what you could not do alone. Allow God to give you a power you do not possess on your own. You may want to read this chapter again and take notes to help understand how to change your old destructive patterns. The next chapter will explain how you can overcome the destructive thinking and feeling messages that are continued in adulthood.

PS: Words of encouragement

You may have learned some new information about your emotions and behaviors. You may have discovered some truths about yourself you don't particularly like. Don't be discouraged. What you have learned can be used to begin healthy changes in your thinking, feeling, and behaving. God wants you to feel good about yourself. You need to allow God, family, friends, or professionals into your life to help make the changes you want to make. As you begin to use this information, you will feel more comfortable as you work it into your daily life.

I will instruct you and teach you in the way you should go; I will counsel you and watch over you.
(Psalm 32:8)

135

Chapter 10

Overcoming destructive thinking and feeling messages

Because the Sovereign Lord helps me, I will not be
disgraced. Therefore have I set my face like flint, and
I know I will not be put to shame.
(Isaiah 50:7)

Negative self-judgment is a product of shame and a distortion of your thinking. You are deceived and brainwashed into believing something about yourself that is not true. Shame consumes you with negative thoughts, and makes you believe the positive side of life cannot be reached (at least, not for you). Negative self-judgment destroys your ability to have a joy-filled life. In addition, unforgiveness and unresolved hurts from your past are the padlocks that keep you from opening the door to spiritual and emotional freedom. This chapter will help you find the key to overcoming destructive thinking and feeling messages.

Origins of judgment

If you want to really learn about the origins of judgment you need to look at the original writings of the Bible. When using the Bible as a reference you must remember, "All scripture is God breathed [inspired by God] and useful for teaching, rebuking, correcting and training in righteous-

137

ness, so that the man of God may be thoroughly equipped for every good work" (2 Timothy 3:16,17). In the Old Testament book Genesis, it is written in Chapters one, two, and three that God created the world with man (Adam) and woman (Eve) in the image of God (Genesis 1:27). God not only created us in His image, but also gave us freedom to make our own choices in life. God told Adam and Eve they could have everything, except the fruit from the Tree of Knowledge. Since the nature of man seems to be to want what you cannot have, they decided to take matters into their own hands and chose to disobey God. Adam and Eve's decision to take fruit from the very place God told them not to is where the origins of sin and judgment on man, woman, and the world began. Consequently, judgment is not your personal fault but an inheritance from the generations before you.

Overcoming self-judgment from your past shame

The original Greek word, Krisis, meaning judgment, is defined by W. E. Vine, Vines Expository Dictionary of the New Testament Words (McLean: Macdonald Publishing Company, p. 621), as follows: "Primarily denotes a separating, then, a decision, judgment ...condemnation." Consequently, when you hold judgment on yourself, you are separating yourself apart as a judge, setting condemnation upon yourself. The original Greek noun, Krites, meaning judge, is defined on page 619 of the Vines, as: 'to a judge who is God of all;'...it suggests that He who is the Judge of His people is at the same time their God...the word judge is also used of God in James 4:12, R.V." The verb form, Krino, is defined on page 620 of the Vines as "primarily denotes to separate, select, choose; hence, to determine and to judge, pronounce judgment." The dictionary points out that when there is self-judgment, you are essentially claiming to be God, setting yourself apart from everyone. When judging yourself, you are playing God and condemning the life that God gave to you. Since you are made in God's image (Genesis 1:27), by rejecting yourself, you are rejecting God.

God does not want you to play god by judging yourself, because then you will always be too critical and never be able to see the valuable person that God made in you. You are a valuable person because God made you that way. It was the people in your life who made you feel not valuable. You are good enough because of what Jesus Christ has done for you and what He says about you. "Therefore, since you have been justified through faith we have peace with God through our Lord Jesus Christ, through whom you have gained access by faith into this grace in which you stand. And you rejoice in the hope of the glory of God" (Romans 5:1-2).

God is your Judge

God wants to be your judge to protect you from your own harsh words of judgment. Besides, the judgment on yourself is not yours to make because God is your Creator and your final Judge. "For we must all appear before the judgment seat of Christ, that each one may receive what is due him for the things done while in the body, whether good or bad" (2 Corinthians. 5:10). "For God will bring every deed into judgment, including every hidden thing, whether it is good or evil" (Ecclesiastes 12:14). God is the only Judge and the One who will pronounce judgment upon you in the final days. The good news is that you can be free from this judgment. No matter what you have done or how bad you believe you are, Jesus Christ can take that judgment and condemnation away, forever! "For God so loved the world that he gave His one and only son, that whoever believes in Him shall not perish but have eternal life. For God did not send His Son into the world to condemn the world, but to save the world through Him" (John 3:16, 17). It is important to understand that God gave you His son Jesus Christ because of His love for you. By simply admitting you are a sinner and accepting Jesus Christ into your heart you will be saved and not be condemned. "Therefore, there is now no condemnation for those who are in Christ Jesus, because through Christ Jesus the law of the Spirit of life set me free from the law of sin and death" (Romans 8:1,2).

As your Heavenly Father, God loves you as one of His children. It is the same with your own children. You may not like what they do, but you will still love them and want the best for them. God created you (see the Holy Bible, Genesis 2:7-25) and will always love you no matter who you are, no matter what you have done, or no matter how bad you feel about yourself. "For I am convinced that neither death nor life, neither angels nor demons, neither the present nor the future, nor any powers, neither height nor depth, nor anything else in all creation, will be able to separate you from the love of God that is in Jesus Christ your Lord" (Romans 8: 38, 39). Accepting the love of your Creator will save you from spiritual and emotional patterns of self-destruction. He wants you to reach out to receive help and establish a loving, intimate relationship with Him.

Overcoming the shame nature

Remember the example earlier in the book of how the shame from each statement or hurtful act slowly chipped away at your heart and mind, like an ax slowly chopping away at the base of a mighty oak tree. Chop after chop, the tree began to weaken, until it was unable to stand from the deep cutting wounds. Like a mighty oak tree falling from the cutting of a sharp ax, the verbal, nonverbal, and physical hurts wounded your heart, mind, and soul. As each hurting statement or action chipped away at your heart, your emotions were never the same. You became helpless to fend off judgmental thoughts and comments toward yourself. The emotional memories became imbedded in your heart and mind, to the point you fell into despair, fear, and oppression. You began to judge and doubt your actions and thoughts. No one could change your mind about how you felt. Since you did not know what else to do, you reluctantly began to live with the misery of the shame nature.

You may be that mighty oak weakened by years' worth of shame. Or, you have been so weakened by shame you have fallen to the ground feeling emotionally dead. Your life may be going nowhere, like the lifeless tree fallen to the ground. You may feel stuck, unable to help yourself change. You are at a crossroads in your life. You want to go forward, but the shame is blocking you. Like that fallen oak tree, your life will remain useless until you choose to make something out of it. You can choose your life to feel useless and in turmoil like a tree being cut up for firewood or you can choose to have your life used by a craftsman to be carved into a beautiful piece of art. You can accept God's help to transform you into something beautiful.

You can decide to be free from shame

Now that you have learned about the shame nature, you have a decision to make. You can either continue to be a lifeless chopping block or allow yourself to be carved into a beautiful example of God's craftsmanship. To discover what God has created in you, the destructive messages need to be let go and the truth needs to be allowed to come in. You need to know the following truths:

- **You are a child of God made in His image.** "...for in the image of God has God made man" (Genesis 9:6). You must claim that passage by rejecting what you were conditioned to believe. This means you are good enough because God made you that way. Your image does not depend on what someone else says. Your image is based on what God has done for you and says about you. 'For we are God's workmanship, created in Christ Jesus to do good works, which God prepared in advance for us to do" (Ephesians 2:10).
- **Know that God loves you.** No matter what you have done, God still loves you. He is waiting for you to allow Him to love you. " 'Though the mountains be shaken and the hills be removed, yet my unfailing love for you will not be shaken nor my covenant of peace be removed,' says the Lord, who has compassion on you" (Isaiah 54:10).
- **Know that God forgives you.** No matter what you have done, God still forgives you if you ask for forgiveness. Even if you do not feel you are worthy to be forgiven, God still loves you and is waiting for you to accept His forgiveness. "You are forgiving and good, O Lord, abounding in love to all who call to you" (Psalm 86:5).
- **God wants a close relationship with you as your Heavenly Father.** You are precious to God and He wants to help. You may be wandering in life like you are lost in the desert without a map. You may not know where to turn. You may be following what looks like the right path only to find it is a mirage, giving you false hope. You may be spiritually and emotionally dry. Your Heavenly Father grieves your situation. He is ready and waiting to help you when you allow him into your life. God will show you the way through His Son, Jesus Christ. "Jesus answered, 'I am the way and the truth and the life. No one comes to the Father except through me" (John 14:6). You can find hope. "And hope does not disappoint us, because God has poured out his love into our hearts by the Holy Spirit, whom he has given us" (Romans 5:5). IF you want to know Jesus Christ personally, sincerely pray the following: "Dear God, I realize I am lost without you and I need you to help me find my way. Please come into my heart and guide my life. In the name of Jesus Christ I pray." Let someone close to you know you prayed this prayer.
- **Do not believe the destructive messages that you heard or were told over the years.** Who are you going to believe? The imperfect opinions of people or the truth from the One who created you? "...Jesus said, 'If

you hold to my teaching, you are really my disciples. Then you will know the truth, and the truth will set you free" (John 8:31 32). You do not need to listen to the destructive, negative messages any longer. Instead, open your heart and mind to what God has to say to you. "But he who listens to me will live in safety and be at ease, without fear of harm" (Proverbs 1:33).

You will overcome the shame nature by acknowledging that the destructive messages in your life are all lies. You must let go of those lies by allowing God to bring the truth to your life. You have been unsuccessful in conquering shame because your heart continues to feel the lies – which in turn makes you believe them. You need the surrendering of your heart, mind, and soul to the truth that only God can give you. When you change the past lies you will change your present feeling and belief about yourself. It is not your fault for the abuse and hurtful things others have done to you in the past. Now you must take responsibility to change how you feel by allowing the Master craftsman, God, to help you let go of the shame nature thinking. His truth and forgiveness will clean your heart to give you the freedom to express emotions, clean your mind of the destructive messages, and free your soul of the bondage to the shame nature.

Overcoming destructive thinking messages

To help you understand the origins of your negative and disrespectful messages, answer the following questions:

- **Was I born not good enough because God made me that way or because the sins of the world and the negative messages of the people in my life made me feel not good enough?** If you believe the sins in the world and people influenced what you believe and feel, you are right. The important people in your life influenced what you believed about yourself. If you were repeatedly told the same thing or treated the same way time after time, you would believe it.
- **Were the negative messages I was given by those people right or correct?** (In other words, if they said I was not good enough, did that mean I really was not good enough?) Absolutely not! The fact that another fallible, imperfect person gave their negative impression of you does not make that impression true. It was only their opinion! Consequently, if their opinion was not correct, then why should you

believe it? As a little child, you were extremely influenced by the authority figures in your life. If you had (or have) a controlling caregiver, you were susceptible to the unhealthy influences of that relationship. If you heard something about yourself often enough, you would believe it was true.

You are good enough because God made you that way! God does not make mistakes. "He is the Rock, His works are perfect, and all His ways are just. A faithful God who does no wrong, upright and just is he" (Deuteronomy 32:4). You were created good enough by God because you were made in the image of God. "So God created man in his own image, in the image of God he created him; male and female he created them" (Genesis 1:27). Since God is your maker, whenever you shame and disrespect yourself, you are insulting God. What you believe about yourself should not depend on another person's opinion. Instead, your identity should depend on what God has said and done for you. "...But you were washed, you were sanctified, you were justified in the name of the Lord Jesus Christ and by the Spirit of our God" (1 Corinthians 6:11).

- **Because people in my life treated me with disrespectful negative messages, should I continue to treat myself with disrespectful negative messages?** Absolutely not! You need to make a decision to stop judging yourself and treating yourself with disrespect. What is important to understand is that these messages are all big lies! These lies hurt and destroy any potential of retaining the good things you receive. The lies keep you from feeling good enough to accept the unconditional love from your Heavenly Father and the love from people around you. It is like you curse yourself whenever disrespectful words come out of your mouth. "Out of the same mouth come praise and cursing. My brothers, this should not be" (James 3:10).

This destructive thinking stops you from loving yourself and allowing others to love you. The shame nature holds you back from the ability to be free from the bondage of destructive messages. You must rid yourself of these continuous internal messages of self-judgment and self-blame. You must recognize that the negative messages are lies and give yourself permission to stop blaming and judging yourself. One-way to begin changing is to tell yourself: "Stop, I don't need to think this way," whenever you think a negative message. After having destructive thinking for many years, you will need to regularly repeat this statement to yourself.

Overcoming destructive feelings and discovering the truth

You have felt the same destructive feelings for so long, you believe they are the truth. You may not realize these destructive lies of self-judgment, abandonment, hurt, fear, shame, etc., were created from the unhealthy interactions with others. You will be destined to live with these lies unless you find the truth. Without the truth your adult responses will be limited to the constant triggering of emotional buttons and childlikeness reactions that you have come to know so well. Unless you uncover the emotional lies and destructive feelings that were created from past experiences, you will continue to suffer with these lies the rest of your life.

During situations in your life, you may often have the same annoying emotional buttons triggered with feelings of anxiousness, fear, sadness, hurt, etc. You may have had the same buttons pushed the same way for years and never understood why you reacted that way. If you want to stop feeling the unhealthy feelings and break free from the same unhealthy emotions that continue to invade your life, try something new by allowing God to show you the truth. The only way you can know the truth is to find it from the One who created the truth and gives the truth. "Then you will know the truth, and the truth will set you free" (John 8:32). You can free yourself of these destructive feelings by allowing God to bring you the truth through the following prayers. You can use these prayers any time you want to be free of the unhealthy feelings or thoughts that plague your mind or body. As you pray, allow God to come to your mind to help you discover the answers.

Whenever your emotional buttons are triggered with negative feelings in your mind or body, (i.e., disappointment, fear, panic, hurt, tension, shaking, sadness, rejection, etc.) find a quiet place and pray the following prayers:
*   *God, come into my mind to help me find healing through your truth*
*   While you are feeling the negative feelings, pray, *God, is there any unforgiveness in my life that I need to confess?* If an image or thought comes to mind, ask God what issues you need to forgive or let go. Do

you need to ask forgiveness for something? For example, if you have anger toward someone, God wants to know why you are angry, how angry you are, and that you want to let it go. Next, ask God to take the anger, and ask for forgiveness for the anger (the next section, "Overcoming Unforgiveness" will help in more detail). When you are done, ask the above question again to determine if other issues need to be forgiven. If nothing comes to your mind, continue on.

- When negative feelings are triggered in your mind or body (i.e., tension, hurt, shaking, fear, etc.), discover the origin of your emotional response by praying:

God, help me find where I learned these childlike feelings.

As you pray, think about past memories with people or circumstances where you may have experienced these feelings. If a memory comes to mind, find the destructive message that you started to believe as a result of that memory, by praying:

God, what destructive message was I told or did I feel? (i.e., I'm not good enough; I can never do anything right, it was my fault, I was afraid, I was not loved; etc.) If past memories or destructive messages do not come to mind at first, continue to pray to God for answers. You may want to find someone to pray with you or pray for you. Watch and listen for answers in your thoughts, feelings, and circumstances. To help stir up memories, talk about your past with someone who is familiar with your background.

- When you discover a destructive message from the past, allow God to help you destroy that lie by praying:

God, take away this feeling of ("name the feeling") and help me find the truth.

Allow God to help you let go of the childlike destructive messages and believe the truth about your adult feelings and circumstances. For example, if you have lived for years with the destructive message of "not feeling good enough," it may be difficult to see, hear, or feel positive messages about yourself. You may find reassurance by praying with someone and receiving help to distinguish between the learned destructive messages of the past and the positive messages that are true about yourself or your circumstances.

- Build a strong foundation by allowing God to bring healthy thoughts, feelings, and actions into your life by praying:

God, help me respond differently to my feelings.

Watch and listen for God to work as you regularly pray for His guidance to help toward healthy thoughts, feelings, and lifestyle changes. Review the section in Chapter Nine about building a firm foundation with healthy living habits. Focus on using the steps found in Chapters Eight and Nine to improve your ability to identify and express feelings. You may want to talk with someone to help you pray and learn the difference between healthy and destructive thoughts, feelings, and lifestyles.

During this process, if your mind goes blank or you have difficulty receiving answers, don't give up. You may be emotionally shutting down from not wanting to remember a hurtful past; not being comfortable with feelings, or not being accustom to sensing the positive messages and truth that God wants for your life. Other reasons for your mind blocking feelings and thoughts may be from issues related to unresolved sin, unforgiveness, or deep anger and resentment that may be in your life. You need to confess these things over to God (the next section will address this issue in detail). He is ready and waiting to take them from you. At any time when you experience negative feelings, the aforementioned prayers will help you let go of the destructive messages and discover the truth that only God can bring. If you still have difficulty thinking of past memories or finding the truth about destructive messages, don't be discouraged. It may be hard to allow memories or feelings to flow freely, especially if your memories and feelings have been distorted or suppressed over the years. Continue to regularly use the set of questions in Chapters Eight and Nine to become familiar with finding and understanding your feelings. As you become more comfortable expressing feelings, you will be better equipped to identify and let go of suppressed emotions. It may be helpful to meet with a Christian counselor to assist with finding the truth.

Overcoming unforgiveness

In the previous chapter you read that unforgiveness was like a cancer that festers inside your body. Hurts that are buried take root in your heart. Every time you suppress more hurts the cancer roots grow deeper and deeper. Unforgiveness multiplies like cancer cells taking control of the mental, physical, and spiritual areas of your life. For healing to begin you need to stop the cancer growth with a healthy dose of forgiveness. When you do not forgive, the pain and torment continues. The only way for you to release yourself from the past is to forgive those that originated the hurt. "Get rid of all bitterness, rage and anger, brawling and slander, along with every form of malice" (Ephesians 4:31). This is not as impossible as you feel. Do not let your negative feelings get in the way of your accomplishing something positive for your life. This section will help you through the process of forgiving God, others, and yourself.

• Forgiving God

If you are like many people who have struggled with abuse and hurtful relationships, you struggle with your relationship with God. It is hard to admit you have questions about His motives and felt hurt, resentment, even unforgiveness toward God. Your thoughts have been like spoiled food that has spread throughout your soul ruining any good that may have come from your relationship with Him. Before you can ask God for His forgiveness, you need to let go of any unforgiveness toward Him. This is a task you can accomplish with His help. You need to know that God is a merciful Heavenly Father and should not be compared to your earthly father. God loves you and understands what you have gone through better than you could ever realize. "And the prayer offered in faith will make the sick person well; the Lord will raise him up. If he has sinned, he will be forgiven" (James 5:15).

God is a forgiving Heavenly Father. "…You are a forgiving God, gracious and compassionate, slow to anger and abounding in love. Therefore you did not desert them," (Nehemiah 9:17). You must make a decision to forgive in order for you to be forgiven. "When you stand praying, if you hold anything against anyone, forgive him, so that your Father in heaven may forgive you your sins" (Mark 11:25).

1. Ask God to help you forgive Him. Just talk to God about how you have thought or felt in the past and what you think or feel now. Ask God for forgiveness for feeling that way, and ask for help to let the feelings go. As a loving God, He will hear and forgive whatever you tell Him.

2. Thanking God. As you thank God for listening and forgiving you, ask Him for help to always remember His forgiveness. Don't take back what you have given to God.

- **Forgiving others**

    The unforgiveness you have for others and yourself has probably festered with deep, ugly roots, like the spreading of a disease. You have a choice: you can continue to live in the torment of the past and let the disease fester out of control or you can let go of the past and be free from the bondage of torment and unforgiveness. "If we confess our sins, he is faithful and just and will forgive us our sins and purify us from all unrighteousness" (1 John 1:9). God desires you to forgive others in order for Him to forgive you. "Be kind and compassionate to one another, forgiving each other, just as in Christ God forgave you" (Ephesians 4:32). You are not alone. Just ask God to help you forgive others and yourself.

1. Write the names of people who have hurt you that you need to forgive. Make a second list of the people you have hurt or things you have done that you need to ask for forgiveness. Before you write, ask God to guide you to the names and specific hurts you have inflicted on others or the hurts suffered from others. Take your time to pray and allow God to guide your heart. This should not be a quick exercise. Do not be afraid to admit what you think or feel.

2. Make a decision to forgive each person for what they have done. You may think, "I cannot forgive this person for what he did to me." You do not have to do this alone; ask God to help you. However, you must earnestly desire for the forgiveness to take place. You may not feel like forgiving the person right now. However, by choosing not to forgive, you are choosing to live with hurt. In essence, you are allowing the other person to continue tormenting you, although you may believe the person was guilty for what happened and that forgiveness does not change the fact that they are wrong. Regardless of what happened, you need to take responsibility to change your own life and healing your own hurt. By choosing to forgive, you are taking control and choosing to move forward toward healing.

3. Find a quiet place where you can communicate with God. Take your list of names and pray the following over each name (If you cannot forgive the person on your own, ask God to help you forgive):

- **For each person who has hurt you:**
    Forgive each person for what they have done or the hurt they have caused. For example, "God, I forgive (name of person) for what they have done."
    Begin letting go of the negative feelings toward each person. For example, "God, help me let go of how I feel about (name of person)."
    Thank God for His forgiveness.

- **For the people you have hurt:**
    Ask God for forgiveness for each person you have hurt. For example, "God, forgive me for: (describe what you did).
    Thank God for being a loving Heavenly Father and forgiving you.
    Ask God what you should do with each person or circumstance to rectify the issue.

4. To help you let go of these hurts; you may want to take the original lists and tear them into tiny pieces. Give yourself permission to be forgiven by God and to be free from the offenders and offenses.

Forgiveness is a belief, not a feeling

When you have shame in your life, you do not believe you are good enough or deserving enough to be forgiven. You are so use to believing you are unworthy that you may not feel forgiven, after you ask for forgiveness. Your shame nature has distorted your inner truth, not allowing you to believe you are forgiven. Your old feeling of being undeserving of anything good in your life makes it difficult to let go of your unforgiveness. The truth is, when you sincerely ask forgiveness from God His forgiveness is immediate. You need to remind yourself, over and over again, that you are forgiven and God's forgiveness is complete. Do not let the old destructive pattern of negative messages stop you from believing you are forgiven. Do not rely on your feelings to determine whether you are forgiven. Rely on the truth from the word of God. "There is now no condemnation for those who are in Christ Jesus, because through Christ Jesus the law of the Spirit of life set me free from the law of sin and death" (Romans 8:1, 2). I remember a bumper sticker that I once saw, which sums up how you should think, "God Said It, I Believe It, That Settles It!"

Overcoming oppression

When you are oppressed there is little room for joy in your heart. You need to fill your heart, mind, and soul with the goodness of life to rid the darkness of shame. Jesus Christ is the light and the forces of evil are the darkness. "When Jesus spoke again to the people, he said, 'I am the light of the world. Whoever follows me will never walk in darkness, but will have the light of life" (John 8:12). You have every right to have a joy-filled life. But first you must get rid of the darkness and gloom that may be consuming you. Jesus Christ died for you so that you may be saved from spiritual death and worldly darkness. "For he has rescued us from the dominion of darkness and brought us into the kingdom of the son he loves," (Colossians 1:13). The following are meant as guidelines to find freedom from the oppression in your life.

- **Know whom you are fighting against.** Oppression is the forces of evil battling against you. You do not need to be afraid. If your heart has accepted Jesus Christ, you have already won the war. You just need the correct weapons to fight the battles. As long as you live in this world you are living in Satan's territory. As long as your heart belongs to Jesus you do not belong to the world. The truth is, if you have not accepted Jesus Christ, you belong to the world.
- **Know Jesus Christ personally.** If you have not been able to overcome the symptoms of oppression by now, the only way you can is through the power and strength of Jesus Christ. The only way to receive that power is to know Jesus as your personal Savior.
- **Cleanse your life of hurts and offenses.** Unresolved hurts, unforgiveness, and an unrepentant heart are the welcome mat for the darkness of demonic forces to steal your joy. You can ask for forgiveness from others and yourself. If you are ready to be serious about your freedom from oppression, follow the same guidelines under the aforementioned section "Overcoming unforgiveness," before moving on.
- **Believe in the saving Blood of Jesus Christ and the Power of the Holy Spirit.** Throughout the New Testament there are examples where

Jesus Christ showed His power over the sickness and evil powers of the world. "Jesus went throughout Galilee, teaching in their synagogues, preaching the good news of the kingdom, and healing every disease and sickness among the people" (Matthew 4:23). As a believer you have the same power over the anguish and offenses of the past, or whatever else keeps you in the darkness of oppression. Jesus gives you the power of the Holy Spirit as He did in the examples of the disciples. "He called his twelve disciples to him and gave them authority to drive out evil spirits and heal every disease and sickness" (Matthew 10:1). Through the power of Jesus Christ you have the authority to overcome oppression. "I have given you authority to trample on snakes and scorpions and to overcome all the power of the enemy; nothing will harm you' (Luke 10:19).

- **Prepare yourself for daily battles.** Once you begin to overcome destructive feelings and discover the truth of the past hurts, the war is not over. You must guard yourself for the rest of your life to continue winning battles. "Finally, be strong in the Lord and in his mighty power. Put on the full armor of God so that you can take your stand against the devil's schemes" (Ephesians 6:10, 11). Thoughts of self-doubt and self-judgment will continue to find ways to creep into your mind. Remember, your adversaries, the demons, are trying to deceive you. You must increase thoughts of the Light (Jesus Christ) to decrease the outside forces of the darkness. There is no darkness (lies) where there is light (truth). "But you are a chosen people, a royal priesthood, a holy nation, a people belonging to God, that you may declare the praises of Him who called you out of darkness into his wonderful light" (1 Peter 2:9). The following are guidelines that can be used on a daily basis to help overcome the spiritual battles in your life:

1. Pray in everything you do. "Pray continually; give thanks in all circumstances, for this is God's will for you in Christ Jesus" (1 Thessalonians 5:17, 18). Prayer is communication with God. He wants to know everything that you are thinking, feeling, and needing. "Do not be anxious about anything, but in everything, by prayer and petition, with thanksgiving, present your requests to God. And the peace of God, which transcends all understanding, will guard your hearts and your minds in Christ Jesus" (Philippians 4:6, 7). You are strongly encouraged to find a partner to pray with on a daily or weekly basis.

2. Read the truth. The word of God is another way that God communicates and guides you. "Your word is a lamp to my feet and a light for my path" (Psalm 119:105). The word of God is also a very powerful weapon against the schemes of the devil. Jesus used scripture when He battled against Satan. "I tell you the truth, if anyone keeps my word, he will never see [spiritual] death" (John 8:51). Get a daily devotional booklet to help you stay in the word each day. You are strongly encouraged to find a Bible study and/or Bible partner to study scripture once per week. Most local churches will have free daily devotionals and information about Bible studies.

3. Go to church regularly. You need to stay in fellowship with a church that teaches from the Bible and believes in the salvation of Jesus Christ. It is important that you worship, pray, and have fun with fellow believers. Allow your fellow believers to pray for you as you pray for them. "But if we walk in the light, as he is in the light, we have fellowship with one another, and the blood of Jesus, his Son, purifies us from all sin" (1 John 1:7).

4. Accept God's inner healing and continue to forgive others and yourself for things that happen. Life will be full of ups and downs that will need constant release through prayer and forgiveness. Use the steps you previously learned to identify and stop the destructive feeling messages that plague you on a daily basis. Allow yourself to trust God to handle the small things while you let go of the larger problems through prayer.

5. If you continue to find oppression overwhelming you, take those signs seriously. There is no reason why you should be oppressed. You may want to continue the healing process with a Christian therapist who is familiar with the struggles and healing from oppression. Many have found help through Christian ministries that assist with inner cleansing and healing of oppression.

   Freedom from shame, self-judgment, unforgiveness, and oppression is a time of releasing the hindrances that have kept you away from the joy that God and life have to offer. "...I am sending you to them to open their eyes and turn them from darkness to light, and from the power of Satan to God, so that they may receive forgiveness of sins and a place among those who are sanctified by faith in me" (Acts 26:17,18). You need to allow the Holy Spirit to increase and the focus on self-centeredness and your hurtful past to decrease. "He [Jesus Christ] must become greater, I must become less" (John 3:30). The more you fill yourself with goodness, the less room you will have for hurts, unforgiveness, and oppression.

Overcoming shame, judgment, unforgiveness, and oppression is a process that will take time. You can do it because God is on your side and God has already won the war. The more time you spend with God, the more strength you will have to fight the battles. "I can do everything through Him who gives me strength" (Philippians 4:13). God will supply your needs to win the battles. "And my God will meet all your needs according to His glorious riches in Christ Jesus" (Philippians 4:19). You must allow yourself to be open to making emotional changes to become the person you desire and the person God wants you to be. The next chapters will begin teaching you how to find the joy of life in ways you have not known before.

PS: Words of encouragement

This may have been a challenging chapter with more information than you expected. Maybe you have been hurt in the past and forgiveness has been on your mind. Maybe the pain seems more than you can handle and you don't think anyone understands what you are going through. You may be painfully aware that God has the answers for your life, with the love and acceptance that you have always wanted. God is waiting for you to open the door to let Him into your life and receive His mercy, compassion, and strength to overcome the hurts in your life. You have the ability to take control of your life and begin the steps to cleaning out old destructive thoughts and feelings. You are on the road to recovery to learn new ways to feel the emotions freely given to you. You can rejoice in what you have accomplished and the healing that will be in store for you ahead.

For I know the plans I have for you,' declares the Lord,
'plans to prosper you and not to harm you, plans
to give you hope and a future.
(Jeremiah 29:11)

Chapter 11

Gauging your feelings

I will give you a new heart and put a new spirit
in you; I will remove from you your heart of stone
and give you a heart of flesh.
(Ezekiel 36:26)

If someone were to give you an eight ounce glass filled with four ounces of water, how would you describe it? Would you say the glass was "half full" or would you say the glass was "half empty?" What if someone asked you to describe how you feel about your life? Would you say you feel good about yourself and good about your life? Or do you feel like there is a black cloud hanging over your head, as if you cannot do anything right? Do you think positive thoughts about your life? Do you feel good about what you do? Or do you think negative thoughts and often feel something bad may happen? The point I am trying to make is, what you feel and believe about yourself will greatly influence how you emotionally respond to daily situations and determine your outlook on life.

Your feelings are preset from the past.

When a gauge is made in the factory it must be preset, or what the industry calls calibrated, to show the correct standard of measurement on the gauge. If the gauge is to show twenty pounds of steam pressure, the factory must calibrate the gauge to accurately show the specific measurement of twenty pounds. Growing up in a home with shame or being treated by a spouse with shame is like presetting or calibrating your inner Feelings Gauge to the feelings that shame brings. When you lived in a home where you did not feel good enough and the majority of what you heard was negative comments, you became accustomed to those feelings and negative words. Consequently, you became accustomed to living around negative people with their daily negative comments and you became accustomed to having emotional buttons triggered with negative feelings. When your life was filled with negativity, you expected negativity. In a home filled with shame, your inner Feelings Gauge was calibrated or set on the shame side of the gauge. You believed it was normal to have negative comments and feeling not good enough. You became comfortable dealing with negativity and felt uncomfortable with praise or compliments. For example, as an adult, if you received positive comments you would believe something was wrong. You may desire compliments and praise, but they were foreign to you. You did not know what to say or feel when compliments or praise came your way.

The result of shame nature is like an anchor around your neck. You may feel so burdened with a deeper sense of unhappiness that obtaining happiness and becoming good enough would not seem realistic. You may have shed tears over the frustration of experiencing problems that seem to keep you from obtaining or maintaining a feeling of happiness. Sometimes you may have periods of happiness that don't seem to last, like a partly cloudy day with the constant threat of rain. Or you may want to feel good, but don't know how to grasp it. One depressed person described wanting to feel good as if someone was holding an ice cream cone right in front of your face, while your hands were tied behind your back. You wanted the ice cream so much you could taste it. Besides, if you had the ice cream cone you could not enjoy it because you would either not feel worthy enough or not know how to enjoy it. That's the same with receiving a good compliment about yourself. You may not believe you deserve it and don't know how to accept it. Not allowing yourself to feel good is a destructive message rooted in shame nature thinking. You are so accustomed to hurtful circumstances in life that create unhappiness, that you doubt your own worthiness to enjoy the happiness and don't feel comfortable when it comes your way. The shame nature thinking in your life has the greatest influence where your feelings are calibrated on your Feelings Gauge. If you were to look at your feelings on a gauge, you would develop a better perspective of the persistent unhealthy feelings and what needs to change to allow healthy feelings to occur.

Discovering your Feelings Gauge

If you can, picture a gauge similar to an automobile fuel gauge with empty on the left and full on the right. Imagining a similar gauge for your feelings, let's find out where your feelings are located on the gauge. This exercise will help you understand how your feelings are influencing your life. As you look at Figure A, let's develop your own inner Feelings Gauge with the saddest moment in your life on the left and the happiest moment of your life on the right. Take a few moments to complete the following steps:

1. In your adult years, come up with a time that you could describe as the saddest moment of your life. On Figure A, write that moment in the space below the words "Saddest moment of your life." Think of the feelings you had during that saddest moment and list that in the area provided beneath the saddest moment. For example did you feel hurt, angry, resentful, painful?

2. In your adult years come up with a time that you could describe as the happiest moment of your life. On Figure A, write that moment in the space below the words "Happiest moment of your life." Think of the feelings you had during that happiest moment and list them in the area provided beneath the happiest moment. For example did you feel free, alive, fun, or happy?

3. On the Figure A gauge, put a dot where you seem to currently feel most of the time.

4. Looking at the dot on the gauge, think about where your feelings tend to fluctuate. Do you feel most often toward the saddest moment side or do you most often feel toward the happiest moment side? With your pen or pencil on the dot, shade the area in the direction toward the moment you tend to feel the most.

Figure A. Feelings Gauge

|_____+_____|

Saddest moment | Happiest moment
of your life: | of your life:

List sad feelings: | List happy feelings:

1. | 1.
2. | 2.
3. | 3.

If you are like many people I see in my office, you feel most often toward the saddest moment side of the gauge. With shame nature it is very normal to feel most of the time toward the sad side of the gauge. This is your comfort zone, and where you have come to believe you are most often expected to feel. Chances are, you do not know how to feel any other way.

Your comfort zone

Your comfort zone makes up those feelings, thoughts, and actions that are the most comfortable to you. When you are in your comfort zone, you feel more in control, safe, and secure. If you have felt the same way most of your life, you develop a sense of strength from knowing you are in your comfort zone. Comfort zones give you a sense of comfort and security believing everything will be the same. You react the same way believing that is the best way to keep the situation from becoming out of control. For example, when emotional buttons are pushed and you become nervous, tense, afraid, unable to think, you are reacting out of your comfort zone, believing something may happen out of your control.

Tara came to see me explaining how she would shut down emotionally whenever someone raised his or her voice. When her husband started to argue, Tara's emotional buttons would trigger extreme nervousness and she would shut down emotionally, wanting to leave. In order to deal with these situations, Tara gave in to her husband's demands, no matter how unreasonable they were. Tara felt taken advantage of by her husband but never felt comfortable doing anything else. She later recalled that her parents' verbal arguments were very scary for her as a child. In the midst of their argument, her father would leave the house. As a child, Tara created an unhealthy belief that bad things happened when people argued. Her comfort zone was to do everything possible to stop people from arguing in the hope nothing bad would happen.

Comfort zones do not let you trust your own feelings

When you grew up in shame the product of that shame thinking became your comfort zone. For example, if you did not feel good about yourself, you did not trust any other feelings. When something good happened in your life, you did not trust the good feeling. You didn't believe it — as if the good feeling was a mistake or some fluke. It was as if you only knew how to feel unworthy, not believing any other way. You didn't trust feeling good, as if it were normal to feel blah and chronically unhappy, like dark clouds were constantly hovering over you. This was common for Mable. She had felt gloomy for years and admitted to not knowing how to feel any other way. During a session, Mable tearfully disclosed traumatic events of the past that were very hurtful. Mable cried for ten minutes as she let go of past mistakes that involved asking God for forgiveness. Mable left the session feeling lighter and happier, as if she had finally let go of a heavy burden. During the drive home, Mable experienced an internal struggle. It was as if an inner voice was telling her, "You didn't really forgive that person. You don't deserve to be happy. You are still wrong, no matter what you do." By the time Mable returned home, she was her gloomy self again. Mable said she was not accustomed to being happy. She felt strange, odd, and did not feel it was right to be happy. She felt as if something was going to happen so she stopped feeling happy. "Feeling happy is not who I am. I don't know how to be happy," she told me at a later session. Mable's comfort zone was clearly that of gloom and no amount of words were going to tell her otherwise. She only trusted the negative feelings that she was conditioned to feel years ago.

When you are out of your comfort zone you feel vulnerable, scared, afraid something will happen or afraid life may become out of control. If you grew up in a home with disorder, chaos, constantly changing rules, and unpredictable feelings from caregivers, you will tend to be more comfortable with an unpredictable way of life or a life where everything must be perfect. If you grew up in a home with relationships that were constantly disrespectful or hurtful, you may tend to be in relationships where there tends to be disrespect and hurt. If you were not allowed to have feelings as a child, you probably would not be comfortable expressing feelings as an adult.

When your comfort zone is closest to the sad moment of your life

When your feelings are most often closest to the saddest moment of life, as shown in Figure B, you are responding to the shame in your life. You are accustomed to not allowing yourself to feel and your comfort zone is to trust the sad and negative feelings that take place in your life. One man who always had feelings on the sad side of the gauge said he felt comfortable in abusive situations, as if he deserved it. As a child, he was not allowed to feel good about what he wanted to do or what he was able to accomplish. This distorted belief continued as an adult.

Figure B. Feelings Gauge

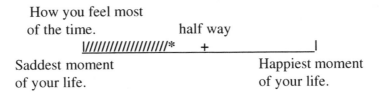

When your feelings are closest to the sad side, you become comfortable with misery. You may not have much experience with lasting joy in your life. Happiness is like a foreign language. You may know a few foreign words, but you do not understand how to speak the language. Similarly, you may have periods of happiness, but you do not know what it is like to have the lasting joy that comes with daily living. When someone in your presence is always joyful, it may make you uncomfortable. If it is not normal for you to feel happy, you may not know what to do with it when it happens. You believe sadness is how you are expected to feel. When you do have periods of happiness, you may automatically feel strange, guilty, or wonder if something bad is going to happen. You may concentrate on when the happiness will end rather than allowing yourself to enjoy the circumstance that makes you feel happy. You are not comfortable with good feelings and you may believe you don't deserve the benefits that happiness brings. Your inner Feelings Gauge only occasionally goes past the halfway mark toward the happiest moment. It is too foreign to feel good and happy for long periods of time. Your Feelings Gauge is calibrated to the sad side, believing that is normal.

When your feelings are closest to the sad side you became comfortable with the triggering of emotional buttons such as sadness and child-likeness reactions. You continue triggering the similar sad feelings that were learned during childhood. While in counseling, Mae said she found it difficult to remain happy for periods of time. She described her parents as having unpredictable explosions of anger, criticism, rules, and demands. Whenever things were going well, her parents would bring up some problem that ruined everything. "It was as if something bad would happen every time I was in a happy mood," she said. If you grew up in a home like Mae, you may not trust having good feelings because you would feel too vulnerable or become afraid something bad might happen when good feelings came your way.

When your comfort zone is on the sad side of the gauge, you keep yourself there by what you say and how you act. Whenever you use destructive messages toward yourself or others, you are continuing the same hurtful methods of shame that calibrated you to the sad side of the gauge as a child. When people in your life repeatedly criticized you for not doing something right, the hurtful message shamed you into believing you were not good enough. That shame calibrated your Feelings Gauge to the sad side of the gauge. As an adult, you continued many of the inner feelings and behaviors that were learned from the experiences as a child. For example, if you criticize yourself for not finishing a project to your liking, you are continuing the shame nature message and keeping the gauge set on the sad side of the gauge. With each criticism, you are telling yourself, "I'm not good enough" or "I don't deserve to be happy." With each self-doubt, self-judgment, and self-criticism, you are sabotaging any chances for good feelings, while keeping yourself on the sad side of the gauge. As one person said to me, "I might as well be sad. I'm going to be that way the rest of my life anyway."

How you should feel most of the time

If your comfort zone is on the sad side of the gauge, you may not be comfortable with happiness for long periods of time. When you have a happy moment, that good feeling may automatically trigger the feeling that something will happen or something is wrong, like a dark cloud hanging over your head. However, life does not need to be lived on the sad side of your gauge. If happiness brings discomfort and thoughts that something is wrong, your gauge needs to be calibrated to a new standard of measurement. Your gauge should be set on the happiest moment side as seen in Figure C.

Figure C. Feelings Gauge

```
                                            How you should feel
                           half way         most of the time.
            I_____+//////////////////////I
      Saddest moment                        Happiest moment
      of your life.                          of your life.
```

God never intended you to live on the sad side of life. Happiness is what you are supposed to feel. God wants you to have joy in your life. "...my joy may be in you and that your joy may be complete" (John 15:11). You do not have to live your life with the results of the shame nature. You may never have known that you are allowed to be happy and feel good about yourself. On the Feelings Gauge, you are supposed to be living somewhere between the halfway mark and the happiest moment of your life. You should have respectful activities in your life that are good, fun, happy, delightful, interesting, pleasurable, and exciting. You deserve to feel good about enjoying every minute of those happy times.

Think about some event or activity in the recent past where you either felt good about something accomplished or an activity you enjoyed. Think of the feelings you had during that moment. If you were having fun and you liked what you were doing, you were supposed to feel that way. If you are accustomed to the sad side of the gauge, you might have become uncomfortable after you felt good. This is the result of the shame nature not allowing you to feel outside your comfort zone of sadness. You must allow yourself to change the Feelings Gauge calibration. When a happy occasion occurs, allow yourself to enjoy that moment. God intended happy feelings to be a normal experience in your life. You are allowed to experience and express the feelings that were freely given to you. Until you discover the truth and let go of the destructive thinking and feeling messages, you will struggle with feeling the joy and happiness that you rightfully deserve.

Your feelings versus the truth

As long as you allow the destructive negative feelings that dominate your mind and heart, you will continue to live on the sad side of the gauge and struggle with resetting your gauge to the happy side. The same negative feelings have been triggered for so long, your reality and logical thinking about good things in life have become distorted. Since you typically trust the negative, you may sabotage your good feelings with destructive messages that make it difficult to separate out your negative feelings from what is the truth or facts. Let me give some possible reasons for your inner struggle between feelings and truth.

The major areas that influence what you believe about yourself are what you feel and what are truth or facts about yourself (this is your logical thinking). First, let's look at the truth (factual or logical) side of you. Think about some household task, professional skill, hobby, talent, or activity that you have performed for some time. When you spend quality time planning your work, you would probably say you know what to do and you can perform that work well. The fact is, logically, you know you can do a good job when you plan and organize your mind to do the task. You know you would do a pretty good job when you put your mind to it. The fact that you have performed well is the truth.

Now let's look at the feeling side of you. Think about that same household task, professional skill, personal hobby, talent, or activity. What would you say if I asked, "After you performed the task, did you feel like it was good enough?" "Did you feel you could have done better?" "Did you feel like you performed well for other people? You may answer these questions saying, "I didn't feel like I did a very good job." Or "I could have done better if I'd practice more." Or, "I'm not as good as Mary. She's really good!" These types of responses indicate you did not feel good about the end result. The difference between using feelings and using facts as the truth is where the confusion starts. When you use negative feelings as your gauge indicator for how well you feel about something, you will distort the facts and truth. Even when the facts show that you did a good job, the negative feeling takes over and distorts your logic and truth. When negative feelings take over, your logical thinking does not work and the facts become useless. You do not see or understand the truth when you allow your negative feelings to become judge and jury about yourself. For example, have you ever received a compliment for your appearance or a talent such as playing a musical instrument, singing, crafts, baking, woodworking, poetry, etc? What did you do with that compliment? Did you feel good about what you accomplished or did you have a difficult time believing it? Since negative feelings bring false impressions and distort reality, you don't allow yourself to believe the fact that you deserved the compliment.

Even when your performance or appearance showed excellent results, the feeling that you could have done better usually wins out. The shame natured person typically has distorted negative feeling that override the fact and truth. The more suppressed hurts you have from the past, the more emotional buttons will trigger those negative feelings and consequently bring more distortion of the truth and logic. You are so accustomed to emotional buttons triggering negative thoughts and feelings, it is difficult to respond any differently; even when you logically know you can perform well. It's as if your logic does not work, only your feelings. One person told me, "I feel like I'm living a lie if I don't go with my feelings. If I don't have the negative feelings, I don't have feelings at all." This person developed a distorted perception of feelings from what was taught in the past. As a result, this person expected the negative to happen, even if it wasn't true. The truth is, if you allow your negative feelings to be your guide, you will continue on a path of hurt and shame, struggling with insecurities and inaccurate feelings that misguide your judgment.

How to identify and change destructive thinking and feelings

People who have lived with shame nature for most or all of their life will find it difficult to recognize that destructive thinking or feeling messages have been triggered. One person asked me, "How do I know when I am using destructive messages, when that is all I've known?" When you have destructive messages you are reacting to the emotional buttons that trigger hurtful me-focused emotional memories or childlikeness reactions.

Often you are reacting from hurtful emotional memories that came from the childhood self-centered and helpless state of mind and body. In other words, you typically react from the feelings of childhood memories rather than what is logically best as an adult for you or others. This me-focused helplessness appears through your thoughts and statements that focus on you, as if nothing else matters. As an adult you may feel or say statements such as:

Nobody loves me.

I don't deserve to feel good.

This is too good to be true.

I don't fit in anywhere.

What is wrong with me?

I can never do anything right.

S/he probably doesn't like me.

I sure messed up on that project!

No one wants to be my friend!

God is punishing me for what I did.

I can't believe I did something so stupid.

I knew something bad would happen to me!

I'm not going to get chosen, I'm not good enough.

Life is so unfair, nothing ever happens good to me.

If they knew the real me, they wouldn't want to talk to me.

Think about any event or activity in the recent past where you can remember enjoying yourself. Think of the feelings you had at the moment you enjoyed yourself. Did you allow yourself to enjoy the activity? Or did you think to yourself, "Something will probably happen. This good feeling will not last"? If something negative happened soon after the fun activity, you may have thought, "I knew it wouldn't last," or "That always seems to happen to me," or "Maybe it's something I'm doing wrong." This type of destructive thinking disrespects yourself and destroys any ability to enjoy what is freely your right to experience. Destructive thinking is the result of negative beliefs and judgments about yourself.

When you are involved in an activity where you feel good, what is the next feeling that comes over you? If negative feelings creep into your thoughts or negative words come out of your mouth that is the shame nature taking over. At that time you must separate yourself from the destructive messages by acknowledging the triggered negative emotions. Begin to listen to the negative statements that come to your mind or come out of your mouth. Have a friend or family member tell you when you are saying negative comments or observing a negative attitude. When you discover these negative statements or feelings, begin the process of identifying the feelings, discovering if they are childlikeness or adult, and finding the truth. Identifying these statements may not be as difficult as you think. The hardest part is allowing someone to help by pointing out your negativity. Changing a lifelong way of negative thinking and feeling is a process, and the peace and happiness in your heart and mind will be the reward.

Tom's story

Tom was one of many managers at a thriving manufacturing firm. He considered himself a hard worker and believed he was feeling good about his work. He stated his work was going well through the past week and he was feeling good about himself. One day he overheard his boss talking about a project with another manager in the next cubicle. Tom overheard his boss giving himself credit for a project that took months for Tom to accomplish. Tom could not believe what he was hearing. His heart sank and he felt a heavy weight on his chest, like a ton of bricks had been dropped on him. He tried to get his mind back to work, but found it difficult to concentrate and did not want to speak to anyone. Tom left work as soon as he could and drove around in his car for an hour before heading home. He became angry as he thought, "That wasn't fair. Why did my boss do that to me? I spent all that time and got no appreciation. I should just quit."

During the evening his wife recognized something was wrong by Tom's angry tone of voice, yelling at the kids, and disrespectful attitude. Using the feelings identification questions (detailed in Chapter Eight), his wife asked, "What's going on inside? Is there something bothering you?" Since Tom was aware of the questions, it made him realize his emotional buttons were triggering an unhealthy attitude. Tom calmed down and began to explain the situation at work. Since his wife was aware of Tom's difficulty with identifying feelings, she asked, "What did the situation make you feel?" Tom recognized his emotional buttons were pushed, but could not recognize the triggered feelings. With the help of the faces on the feelings chart, Tom was able to identify hurt, disrespect, and anger as the feelings that came over him. When his wife asked the question, "Why are you feeling that way," Tom was able to describe in more detail how unfairly he felt the boss had treated him.

Since Tom was not accustomed to identifying his inner feelings, he wanted to make sure this emotional reaction was appropriate for the situation. Tom decided to find out if he reacted with a childlikeness reaction or an adult response (detailed in Chapter Nine). He asked himself, "Was there anything I've done wrong to make me feel this way? After recalling the comments made by his boss, Tom believed there was nothing he did wrong at work for him to react the way he did. With the help of his wife Tom asked, "Did I respond with a childlike reaction or an adult reaction? Tom realized his emotional buttons had automatically triggered me-focused reactions of an emotional shut down at work with a subsequent angry reaction when he returned home. Although Tom didn't like to admit it, he recognized the me-focused, self-centered reactions triggered his emotions that were more like a childlikeness reaction. Tom asked the next question, "Did I need to feel this way?" His wife helped him look outside himself to what was going on around him. Tom realized he was allowed to feel angry and hurt as an adult, but should not allow the me-focused reaction of emotionally shutting down or the outburst of anger. Next, Tom asked, "How should I respond as an adult?" Tom realized he should be allowed to identify how the incident made him feel and express those feelings with his wife and boss. Tom decided to write a letter to his boss to explain his disapproval of the situation. These questions helped identify his helpless childlikeness reactions and learn more appropriate and productive adult ways to handle the situation.

From this situation at work, Tom began to realize that whenever people in authority challenge his accomplishments the emotional buttons trigger an extreme tightness or heaviness in his chest. Tom decided to find out the truth about these feelings and stop the unhealthy reactions. He wanted to find any destructive messages that may have been causing these unhealthy feelings (detailed in Chapter Ten). Tom found a quiet place and prayed, "God, come into my mind to help me find healing through your truth. " Tom started by asking, "God, is there any unforgiveness in my life that I need to confess?" As he was sitting quietly, the angry comments he said to his children came over his mind. He asked God for forgiveness and planned to apologize to his children and wife. Next, as Tom thought about his work situation, he realized that work was a trigger for the familiar feelings of heaviness in his chest. Next, he asked, "God, where in my life did I learn these feelings." After some time Tom remembered how often his father stood over him with a stern, demeaning voice. From those experiences he realized the destructive message was that no matter how much he tried, it was as if he couldn't do anything right, especially for his father. He then began to pray, "God, take away this feeling of not being good enough and help me find the truth" After much prayer and thought, Tom realized he was good enough as an adult and did not need to continue the destructive feelings of "not being good enough," that originated in his childhood. Finally, Tom prayed for guidance, "God, help me respond differently to my feelings." Over the subsequent days and weeks, Tom began to respond more positively as he regularly prayed, read the Bible, and changed how he thought and felt about himself. Tom realized he relied only on his own thoughts and strength to get through situations. He never thought about praying through his situations to allow God to help him.

Like Tom, you may go through hurtful situations but not recognize how they affect you. Tom did not like what happened at work, but he was not aware of how the triggered emotional buttons negatively affected his mind and body. As he allowed the unhealthy responses to continue they festered into reactions that took him more out of control. Like Tom, you can identify emotional reactions and take control of them before they control you. You can take control of the childlikeness reactions, find the truth, and stop unhealthy responses.

You do not need to struggle alone

One benefit your hurting past may have brought you is the ability to rely on your own strength to get through tough situations. The struggles of the past have forced you to become independent and self-reliant in facing problems. You have become more comfortable with being in control to get the job done rather than needing the help of others. On the other hand, as you have become more self-reliant you have a harder time letting others into your life. Your independence has been healthy for your survival, but it has also pushed away the very people who may have been placed in your life to help ease the pain or reduce the struggles. You may have a difficult time letting people into your personal life, not trusting them to get emotionally close. You may feel too vulnerable to let others know how you really feel inside because you may be afraid of getting hurt, losing control, or afraid others will not like you. This pattern of excluding others to independently get the job done does not make you wrong or a bad person, it is a destructive habit that does not need to be used any longer.

You may have wanted to make changes in your life, but you never understood why you were unable to make them happen. You may have struggled with your feelings for years, knowing there was something wrong but not being able to describe it or do anything about it. One of the reasons you struggle is because you are trying to change under your own power. You should realize your ability to change is only as good as the knowledge and strength that you possess. You have worked hard and done a good job of surviving up to this point in your life. However, you don't need to only survive anymore. You can be victorious in what you do. One of the ways to be victorious is for you to give up your self-reliant, me-centered thinking, and allow yourself to receive help from others. You need a power greater than yourself and the support of God, family, and friends that can help with lasting change. You need to know that God is committed to helping in your circumstances and desires you to find joy. "You have made known to me the path of life; you will fill me with joy in your presence, with eternal pleasures at your right hand" (Psalms 16:11).

God will help you with the changes as you pray specifically to Him. "My grace is sufficient for you, for my power is made perfect in weakness. Therefore I will boast all the more gladly about my weaknesses, so that Christ's power may rest on me" (2 Corinthians 12:9). Now that you know the unhealthy influence of negative feelings and destructive thinking, you need to take responsibility to change. This will not be an easy change, especially if this is the only way you know how to think and feel. However, you do not need to go through this alone. God is on your side and He wants you to be healed, just as you desire to be healed. The next chapter will give you wisdom how to find the joy that you deserve.

PS: Words of encouragement

You may never have realized that sadness was so great in your life. Being asked to change the way you are may seem like being asked to move a mighty mountain with only a small hand shovel. Do not let the old destructive messages get in the way of what you can do with the help of Almighty God. As you seek help from others and take control of your feelings you will change the calibration of your Feelings Gauge.

He gives strength to the weary and increases the power to the weak.
(Isaiah 40:29)

Chapter 12

Bearing fruit in your life

You did not choose me, but I chose you and appointed you
to go and bear fruit – fruit that will last. Then the
Father will give you whatever you ask in my name.
(John 15:16)

Many people I see in my office describe sensations of being over-whelmed, weighted down, confused, discontent, empty, or feeling like a dark cloud is hanging overhead. If it is your tendency to allow daily hurts and negative emotions to accumulate within you, the overflow of emo-tional memories will not allow room for the deeper feelings of peace and joy in your heart, mind, and soul. One way to help understand this is to imagine putting garbage into a kitchen trash container until there is no more room. If you are like me, you keep pushing the trash down because you don't have time to empty the container. Eventually there will be no more room and the garbage will overflow. If you leave it long enough, it will begin to rot and stink! Now think of the accumulation of hurts, disap-pointments, sadness, and anger you've had in your heart. If you were not allowed to let go of those hurts, they would continue to pile up, making it necessary to repeatedly push them down to make room for more. Over the years those disappointments and hurts would begin to affect you just like the stinking garbage. You may be so full of suppressed hurts there is no room for any of the good things in life such as love and lasting joy. You have so much emotional garbage packed inside that you are stuck on the sad side of your Feelings Gauge with no room for lasting joy in your heart.

Your life may have momentary periods of happiness that give you a false sense that everything is fine. However, that can be like a long roller coaster ride where your emotions are up and down depending on the circumstances of the moment. You may see other people look happy and wonder why you lack what they have. Deep inside you may shrug off the thought of ever having happiness, believing it was not meant for you. Unfortunately, you are not alone in your desire to want happiness. You have every right to feel peace of mind and a sense of joy in all situations. You should have a sense of lasting peace about your circumstances or deeper sense of joy, regardless of the disappointment. The only difference between the person who has joy and your lack of joy is that you did not receive the foundation of security and safety earlier in your life to learn how to receive and maintain love, peace, and joy.

Annie's story

When I first met Annie in my office she described growing up with her family in a "good" home where she remembered having some happy moments. However, she admitted not feeling good about herself and not feeling a lasting contentment about her life. She continued to describe her frequent desire to please her parents, believing she needed to work hard to be good enough. She searched for happiness with her friends but only found disappointments in what they said and did to her. She searched for satisfaction in the material things she bought and the gifts she received but eventually the excitement of owning things would fade. As the years went by, she noticed an increasing inner emptiness that she could not understand. After high school she decided to continue on with more education, believing filling her head with knowledge would make the difference. As the years pushed on, she realized the education only proved that she was getting smarter in the head with little to fill her heart. She frequently thought about finding the right mate, in the hope it would fill that emptiness within her. She looked for satisfaction in life through daily activities and material things only to find them disappointing. As an adult, Annie did not like having periods of anxiety that kept her awake at night. Nor did she like the worries about her unknown future. Annie wanted peace of mind and lasting joy that would continue no matter what the circumstances. With the help of some friends, Annie realized she was not alone in how she felt and she was not going to find happiness from her own accomplishments.

Annie's desire for satisfaction in life and lasting joy is like having a tall drinking glass in your hand and needing it filled with cool, refreshing water on a blistering hot day. Think of the empty glass as your soul and the cool refreshing water as the satisfaction and joy in your life. Annie spent her life looking for various fancy drinking glasses to be sure there was something good enough to hold the refreshing water. She was so busy finding her reassurance in the things to hold the water, she did not consider looking for the source that would satisfy her thirst. She never realized there was an abundance of thirst quenching water through a relationship with knowing Jesus Christ. "Whoever drinks the water I give him will never thirst. Indeed, the water I give him will become in him a spring of water welling up to eternal life" (John 4:14). If only Annie had known that Jesus was the source of joy for her life.

Like Annie, you may want to experience the fruits of lasting joy and the calming peace in life. You search for it through things, people, places, and trying to be good enough in whatever you say or do. Even the Bible addresses the fact that you will be disappointed from relying on worldly things. "Do not store up for yourselves treasures on earth, where moth and rust destroy, and where thieves break in and steal. But store up for yourselves treasures in heaven, where moth and rust do not destroy, and where thieves do not break in and steal. For where your treasure is, there your heart will be also" (Matthew 6:19-21). Hopefully you have come to realize that dependence on the things and people of the world will not bring you the fulfillment in life you may be looking for. People will eventually disappoint you and things will eventually break or wear out. You want to experience the peace and joy that come from a sense of security, believing everything will work out regardless of what happens. How are you seeking contentment and joy in your life? Are you drinking God's abundant water of joy and eternal life? It is free to you when you ask Jesus Christ to come into your life. He will take care of the abundant supply of living water that will help you bear the good fruit in life.

Filling your life with the fullness of joy

If you are like me, you want to experience the good fruits of life such as love, joy, inner peace, patience, kindness, a good heart, faithfulness, gentleness, and a feeling of being in control. Experiencing these may be foreign to you, as if you have only read about them or seen them in other people. The truth is these are available to everyone, even you! However, deep inside you may think of yourself as a bad apple on a diseased fruit tree. You may think, "How can I experience good fruits when I feel bad about myself?" As you have learned earlier in the book, your destructive thinking will not allow you to see the potential of your own life and what fruit you can bear. As you change how you think and feel, you can begin to bear the fruits of life. Let's begin to learn what you can do to obtain these fruits in your own life.

If you are like most people I speak with, you want to feel the fullness of life. Not a fullness of dissatisfaction with an empty heart, but a fullness of contentment with a heart of peace and joy. Jesus tells you, "... my joy may be in you and that your joy may be complete" (John 15:11). Jesus wants you to experience a joy that is full and complete. Not a momentary joy that only comes when something good happens and shortly disappears. But a peace of mind that remains even with circumstances that you have little control over. You want to be reassured with a power greater than yourself that can help you be secure, regardless of the circumstances. You also want the reassurance that the situation will work out for your best even if you do not get what you want. There is a fullness of inner peace that only a relationship with Jesus Christ can provide beyond what you can do for yourself. This is a joy only Jesus can give to you as you learn to trust Him and find yourself secure in what He has already done and will continue to provide for you. You must remember that the statements in the Bible about what God will do are more than mere statements; they are promises that you can hold onto through all circumstances. No matter what happens, there is reassurance Jesus will be there. Jesus said, "And surely I am with you always, to the very end of the age" (Matthew 28:20).

God wants you to have the best that life can offer, which includes a relationship where He can help you obtain the fruits you just read about. God knows you have a desire to feel the joy of life, because He is the creator of that joy and wants to give it away to you. However, you may not be accustomed to asking or receiving good messages from others. If you came from a shame-filled home you were given negative messages that made you feel uncomfortable with positive things. You must not compare the goodness of God with the negative authority figures in your life. God wants to give away what you need as you are ready to receive it. Jesus tells you to ask for that joy, "Until now you have not asked for anything in my name. Ask and you will receive, and your joy will be complete" (John 16:24).

You can overcome life's troubles

Jesus also knows that the world is full of diversions, disappointments, troubles, and hurts that get in the way of allowing you to obtain the joy in life. Jesus says, "I have told you these things, so that in me you may have peace. In the world you will have trouble. But take heart! I have overcome the world" (John 16: 33). Even two thousand years ago Jesus talked about having troubles in the world just as He is aware that you will have troubles now. When Jesus states you may have peace, He is referring to the choice to accept Jesus into your heart and allow Him to help you. If you do not choose the help of Jesus, you will be left alone to struggle for yourself. When Jesus says, "In the world you will have trouble," He is warning that the world will give you troubles. You may have plenty of experience with trouble and even Jesus knows your difficulties in life will continue. However, Jesus Christ cares enough to let you know He has already overcome the world. You also have the reassurance of overcoming those worldly troubles if you allow Christ into our life and let Him help you. He says, "Peace I leave with you; my peace I give to you. I do not give to you as the world gives. Do not let your hearts be troubled and do not be afraid" (John 14:27).

Why you have trouble bearing good fruit in life

When you allow Jesus Christ to take over your daily troubles, your mind and heart do not have to be consumed with those struggles that overcome your life. You will divert your mind to allow the daily blessings of peace and joy that only Jesus Christ can bring. To illustrate, I will use the story of the fruit tree that Jesus tells to His disciples in Chapter Fifteen in the Gospel of John. "I [Jesus] am the true vine, and my Father [God] is the gardener. He cuts off every branch in me that bears no fruit, while every branch that does bear fruit he prunes so that it will be even more fruitful" (John 15:1, 2). As with any fruit tree, there are healthy branches that need pruning and unhealthy branches that need to be cut away. For example, unhealthy branches that are diseased or dead are best removed to fend off the potential of disease and allow healthier growth to the other branches.

Healthy branches growing in the wrong direction need to be pruned since they sap the vital nutrition out of the tree, interfering with healthy growth. Fruit trees need to receive proper nurturing with water, fertilizer, pruning, and protection in order to yield a healthy crop.

If you were to picture your life like a fruit tree, what would you see? Do you see a life of dead and diseased branches with shame, self-judgment, unresolved hurts, and unforgiveness? Do you have habits or relationships that are like branches growing in the wrong directions that are sucking the vital life out of you? Like the tree, life may be diseased from the inside, choking out life with little clear direction. As a result, you will not bear healthy fruit. What do you feel most of the time? Are you dying from the inside out? Are you choked with troubles, unforgiveness, poor relationships, and destructive habits that are like dead or diseased branches in your life? Do you have difficulty finding the right direction or purpose for your life? Do the unhealthy feelings and destructive thoughts fester inside like a disease? Are you involved in activities that make you feel guilty? Do you have unforgiveness toward yourself, God, or others? Do you have talents and skills that can be used by God? Has your life been as fruitful as you would like it to be? You may want to bear good fruit, but you have not been given the right methods of nurturing, pruning, and caring for yourself to develop the type of good, productive life that you desire. You have the opportunity to make the changes to bear healthy fruit in your life.

Receiving the fullness of life

When you properly care for a fruit tree you will produce the best quality fruit. The same is true for your life. When you properly care for yourself, you will receive the fruits of your labor. The Bible reassures you of this in Galatians 5:22,23. "But the fruit of the Spirit is love, joy, peace, patience, kindness, goodness, faithfulness, gentleness, and self-control. Against such things there is no law." As a child of God, you are eligible to receive what He created for you. All Jesus asks is that you accept Him and follow Him as your daily guide and example. As you draw closer to Him, the fruit will be a result of your growing relationship. "Whatever you have learned or received or heard from me, or seen in me—put it into practice. And the God of peace will be with you" (Philippians 4:9). In order to find the lasting joy and bear the fruit of the Spirit you need to be like Jesus

Christ. "...then make my joy complete by being like-minded, having the same love, being one in spirit and purpose. Your attitude should be the same as that of Christ Jesus" (Philippians 2:2, 5). As you get to know Jesus as your friend, He will help you be more like Him in thought, word, and deed. To properly cultivate your life to bear healthy fruit, you need to surrender the way you care for your life and allow Jesus to be your gardener.

In order to receive the fullness of healthy thoughts and feelings, you need to allow Jesus Christ to help you nurture, fertilize, prune, and protect your life. If you are a gardener or fruit grower, you know the work involved with growing healthy plants. You also know the rewards and satisfaction you receive from seeing healthy plants grow. With anything you do, remember, "Whoever sows sparingly will also reap sparingly, and whoever sows generously will also reap generously" (2 Corinthians 9:6). God wants you to cultivate a relationship with Him in order that you will receive the fullness of His fruit. Let's look at ways you can bear healthier fruit.

Nurture yourself.

Since God is your creator, it only makes sense to have Him involved with your nurturing. To know about these fruits you need to know about Jesus. In order to know about Jesus, you must have a relationship with Him. In order to have a relationship with Jesus Christ, all you need to do is ask Him into your heart. Once you ask Him into your heart, allow His nurturing to take place. Without the nurturing power of the one who created you, it will be harder to heal and grow. "I am the vine; you are the branches. If a man remains in me and I in him, he will bear much fruit; apart from me you can do nothing" (John 5:5). God wants to be involved in your search for joy. We must allow Jesus into our heart and ask specifically for the joy. Jesus wants you to be specific in your prayers and He wants you to trust Him to wait for the answers. Do not look for the answers in the usual ways. After you pray, listen for answers from quiet thoughts and look for answers through scripture reading, and what happens with people and circumstances. Your heavenly Father knows what you need far better than you do. He will give you the desires of your heart, as you are ready for them.

Allow yourself to live on the happy side of your Feelings Gauge. Do not continue the destructive messages struggling to enjoy life. Over the years, people and circumstances created the shame nature thinking and behaving. You can make the decision to treat yourself the way you believe you should be treated and the way you have always wanted to be treated. Be kind to yourself by treating yourself to something that you will enjoy and allow the time to enjoy it. Go to a movie, read a fun book, go out to lunch, do something fun. Allow yourself to have a good time. When you are having a good time with friends, allow yourself to feel good, without fear or concern something will happen. When it's time to go home, re-member, you are allowed to carry home that good feeling. Do not let the past get in the way of you enjoying what life has to offer. Remember, if you become upset or lose that good feeling, respect yourself by identifying what you feel by asking the following questions (detailed in Chapter Eight):

- What is going on inside of me?
- What do I feel right now?
- Why do I feel this way?

After you find your feelings, you may not know if your feelings or behaviors were appropriate for the situation. You can use these simple questions (detailed in Chapter Nine) to uncover the appropriate feeling or reactions.

- Is there anything that I have done wrong that caused me to feel this way?
- Am I responding with a childlike reaction or adult-like response?
- Do I need to feel this way?
- How can I respond differently?

Fertilize your life

As with a plant, carefully adding extra nutrients will improve the outcome of your efforts. This is also true for the physical, emotional, and spiritual parts of your life. If you want to have a good outcome, you will need to put forth the effort to add the extra nutrients to feed your mind, heart, and soul. You need to continue educating yourself to make the proper changes. For example, you have made an excellent start by reading this book. To receive nutrients to all areas of your life it would be helpful to read other self-help books or a daily Bible devotional (most churches have these available) and attend classes or worship services at a local church. "For the word of God is living and active. Sharper than any double-edged sword, it penetrates even to dividing soul and spirit, joints and marrow; it judges the thoughts and attitudes of the heart" (Hebrews 4:12).

When you hear or read God's word, you will receive powerful nourishment that will brighten your heart, empower your mind, and open your soul to receive the richness of life that is in store for you. His word is a bright light that will penetrate, and cut out the darkness in your heart like a sharp knife. Fertilize your heart, mind, and body by reading the word of God and hearing the word of God through church messages, Bible studies, and music. "Let the word of Christ dwell in you richly as you teach and admonish one another with all wisdom, and as you sing psalms, hymns and spiritual songs with gratitude in your hearts to God" (Colossians 3:16).

Prune your life

Do you have any unhealthy thoughts, feelings, behaviors, habits, relationships, unforgiveness, or lifestyle that needs to be pruned away? Do you have any unhealthy reading material, words, music, videos, television, and behaviors permitted in your life that hinder you from producing healthy fruit? If you do not know whether you have unhealthy habits or lifestyles, you may want to seek Christian counseling, begin reading the new testament Bible (the Gospel of John is a good place to start) and go to a church that focuses on teaching the Word of God. You need to realize pruning is a process. Just like it can be unhealthy to prune too many branches off a tree at one time, it may be unrealistic for you to change all unhealthy behaviors overnight (unless God chooses to). I am not giving you an excuse to continue the unhealthy habits, but a word of caution. You will have difficulty trying to stop a long-term habit on your own. You are expected to daily pursue the goal of cleansing your life, but you need the help of others. Let God, family, friends, or church members know what you are trying to do. Allow them to pray for you and give the habit to God and allow Him to help take it from you and replace it with a healthy lifestyle. Remember, as you discover destructive feeling and thinking messages that keep you in bondage to shame, self-judgment, and self-doubt, you need to prune them away by praying through the following (detailed in Chapter Ten):

• God, is there any unforgiveness in my life that I need to confess?

- God, help me find where I learned these childlike feelings.
- God, take away this feeling of ("name the feeling") and help me find the truth.
- God, help me respond differently to my feelings.

Protect your thoughts and feelings

No matter how strong you may believe yourself to be, you have fleshly weaknesses that will get in the way of bearing the fruit of life. Protect yourself from temptations, negativity, hurts, and unhealthy living. "Watch and pray so that you will not fall into temptation. The spirit is willing, but the body is weak" (Matthew 26:41). Do not put yourself in situations where you will be tempted or fall victim to sin or hurt. For example, if you have problems with negative thoughts or words, stop sitting around with fellow employees, family, or friends who are frequently negative. Negativity breeds more negativity. You need to step back in all situations of your life and look over what is happening. Ask yourself, "Is this situation hindering me from thinking and feeling good about myself?" or "What could I do differently in this situation to improve how I think and feel about myself?" If you have lived in a home with shame, you will have a difficult time changing what you think, feel, and say about yourself. You have been around negativity for so long you will need help to recognize when you are having negative thoughts or feelings. It will be hard at first to allow someone to help you with your changes, but the outcome will be worth the effort. Find a safe person that can be an accountability partner. To help stay true to the changes in your life, meet with someone often to pray and have them ask questions about your thoughts, feelings, habits, or lifestyle.

Just as you protect trees from diseases and infections to yield a healthy fruit, you need to protect yourself from verbal, nonverbal, and physical hurts of others. These hurts have already damaged your heart, mind, and soul and you do not want to allow any more destruction in your life. If you grew up or currently live in a home with shame-natured messages, you will have a harder time recognizing when others give verbal and nonverbal destructive messages. For example, a common complaint I hear is that of a family member returning home from a stressful day of work or after visiting with parents who use shameful messages. The returning family member often takes on the negativism from the work environment or hurtful parents and then passes on the negative attitude to their own family members. If you realize (even if you have always known) your job, caregivers, or spouse were (or currently are) hurtful to you, instead of trying to change them, first work on changing yourself. The best way to change someone else is to first change how you feel and react to others. As you begin to heal yourself, you will be better able to handle the hurts that come your way. The harder you try to forcefully change another person who has been hurtful to you, the more that person will hurt back. If someone is still hurting you, here are some suggestions:

1. Do not put yourself in positions to get hurt. Throughout your life you will find work mates, friends, family, spouse, or elderly caregivers that will be hurtful and oppress your feelings. At first, you may need to keep your distance from hurtful people (of course, this will be harder with your spouse) until you become more confident to be open with your feelings. If they ask why you are distancing yourself, tell them you are making some changes in your life and need time and space to figure things out. Although hurtful people tend to expect you to inform them about everything at all times (it's called "controlling"), you may want to be careful what you initially tell them. If you are able to tell the hurting person details, tell them only as much information as you are comfortable disclosing. Be careful that you do not tell them details that can be turned around and later used against you.

2. Begin to change the situation by changing how you feel and react to the situations. When emotional buttons are pushed, use the questions in this book to identify your feelings and stop the unhealthy responses you experience. Get out your feelings by writing them down, saying them out loud (or in prayer), or with safe people. Find other self-help literature or speak with a professional to learn new ways to handle the hurtful situation. Most importantly, allow yourself the ability to get help and change how you respond to the hurtful messages.

3. Once you become more confident, express your feelings to the person who hurts you. For example, you may say, "It hurts me when you say that. Please don't say that to me any more." If the other person responds with more hurtful statements, chances are, any comments you make will make them more defensive. Regardless of what the hurtful person says, you are allowed to respectfully express how you feel. If you tell them how you feel, their own insecurity drives them to do more of what they do best; and that is to be demanding, controlling, hurtful, and angry. Since they are also hurting and insecure people,

they often use their offensive behaviors as a defense to protect themselves from feeling wrong.

As a single parent who was recently divorced, Jan was making positive strides toward her independence, in spite of the constant criticism from her father and ex-husband. She told me how proud she was for making a decision on buying a car that was much needed for her and her three children. Jan was so happy that she was able to make this first major decision without the help of her father and ex-husband. Although Jan was eager to prove to her father she was strong enough to make decisions on her own, she was nervous about how he would accept her strides toward independence. When she finally called her father and excitedly told him the good news, the first words out of his mouth were, "I can't believe you bought a car like that!" Jan went silent as her heart sank down deep. Any good feelings she was experiencing were suddenly cut off. This response was so common by her father that Jan automatically fell into the childlike state of mind by shutting down her emotion. She did not know what else to say, so she hung up the phone.

As you make good strides in your own life, like Jan, you still may not be ready to deal with the hurtful people around you. You may begin to make emotional changes in your life, but the hurtful people in your life will still be the same. Don't put yourself in a position to be hurt until you are emotionally ready to express yourself, knowing hurtful messages will continue to come your way. Identifying the emotional buttons that trigger childlike reactions and subsequently switching to adult responses is a process. Do not let the destructive shame messages stop you from believing that you can be victorious to making changes in your life. Begin to respect yourself by identifying, expressing, and stopping the destructive messages from destroying you.

You will know a good tree by its fruits

With proper nurturing, fertilizing, pruning, and protection, you will bear the good fruit of love, joy, peace, patience, kindness, goodness, faithfulness, gentleness, and self-control. This fruit will be evident in how you feel, what you think, and how you conduct yourself. You will, in time, develop the Fruit of the Spirit as you develop a closer relationship with Jesus Christ and pattern your life after Him. God desires that you have a fruitful life – living your life to the fullest and experiencing the abundance that life has to offer. "You did not choose me, but I chose you and appointed you to go and bear fruit – fruit that will last. Then the Father will give you whatever you ask in my name. This is my command: Love each other" (John 15:16, 17).

PS: Words of encouragement:

You may have never realized you had the ability to have a good, fruitful life. After years of hurts and turmoil, it may be hard to think of yourself as having inner joy and peace. It may also be hard to realize that God really loves you and wants you to have an abundance of joy in your life. God misses the opportunity to give you that joy through a close relationship with Him. Don't stop yourself from pursuing the Fruit of the Spirit that is free to you. As you continue on the road to recovery you will bear the fruit of your efforts.

And we pray this in order that you may live a life worthy of the Lord and may please him in every way; bearing fruit in every good work, growing in the knowledge of God, being strengthened with all power according to his glorious might so that you may have great endurance and patience, and joyfully giving thanks to the Father, who has qualified you to share in the inheritance of the saints in the kingdom of light.
(Colossians 1:10-12)

Chapter 13

Healing through the truth

*But when he, the Spirit of truth, comes, he will guide you
into all truth. He will not speak on his own; he will
speak only what he hears, and he will tell you what is yet
to come. He will bring glory to me by taking from me what is
mine and making it known to you.*
(John 16:13, 14)

The messages you have heard or felt through your life have been the foundation for your belief system about yourself. The messages told to you by significant people in your life have become the truth that you live by. Dr. Bernie S. Seigel wrote in his book Peace, Love and Healing (New York: Harper & Row Publishers, 1989, p. 84), "The fact is, for better and often unfortunately for worse, we communicate with our inner selves all the time. And so do those around us – especially people in positions of trust, power or authority, like parents, teachers and doctors. We need to make sure that the message that gets through is a healing one." Whatever consistent messages you received have become your belief system and the unhealthy emotional buttons that are triggered become your comfort zone. As a result, you may be so comfortable feeling the same unhealthy way, you remain on the sad side of the Feelings Gauge. If your comfort zone were preset on the sad side of the gauge, any good or positive feeling or message would seem strange, untrue, and uncomfortable.

If you lived (or now live) in a home full of shame messages, you were living on a belief system of lies. The destructive messages you received (or receive) and stored in your heart are all lies. The negative messages you heard in the past and may still be hearing are the destructive messages that became your truth. That distorted truth becomes your reality and nothing else seems to be right. This distorted truth is empty and a false sense of security that is sending you on a path of destruction. You have believed the same inner lies for so long you do not trust the truth. That is why it is hard to trust your own feelings or accept good things from others. As long as you believe those lies, you will be dying a slow death of destruction in shame, judgment, doubt, and oppression. Sadly, if you do nothing to change those lies, you may die never knowing the truth about yourself. You may never know what it feels like to unconditionally be loved or give love to others; to have peace of mind; to have lasting joy; and to believe you are good enough no matter what happens. Most importantly, you would never know what it would be like to easily identify and trust your feelings and be able to freely and safely express those feelings with clarity and confidence.

Living in the truth

It is time you stopped dying in a negative world of lies and start living in a glorious life of truth. The only way you will be free of the painful past, learn to deal with the present, and move on with a glorious future is to know the truth and know where the truth comes from. No one can help you change until you decide you want to know the truth and want to let go of the lies. "...If you hold to my teaching, you are really my disciples. Then you will know the truth, and the truth will set you free" (John 8:31-32). The only way to handle the hurtful verbal, nonverbal, or physical messages that come your way is to stand on the firm foundation of truth. Your ability to see through the lies rests in the strength of that foundation. As a child your foundation of truth was built upon the experiences with others and how you were allowed (or not allowed) to express yourself. Your truth was molded by the quality and appropriateness of those experiences. As you grew up you continued to rely on the same foundation for your truth. Hopefully, you have learned that the early foundation turned out to be full of lies and faulty messages that have impacted every part of your heart, mind, and body.

There was a married couple that dreamed of building their own home. After months of looking for land and just the right floor plans, the couple decided they would take the plunge and contract the building themselves. They spent countless hours finding available contractors to dig the hole for the basement, pour the cement foundation, and begin the wooden structure. They both were busy people consumed in their own occupations, which gave them limited time to communicate with each other, or be available at the building site. After months of frustrations, delays, and sleepless nights, the day finally came when they could move into their new home. It was a long awaited, glorious day. They were excited to actually sleep their first night in the home they had waited so long for.

After their first winter, the ground began to thaw and spring rains began to fall. One day the wife noticed some crack lines in the walls of two bedrooms. She frantically called her husband who anxiously contacted the builder. The builder shrugged it off saying there was nothing to worry about since it was a new house and bound to do some settling. Although the husband was not totally relieved, he felt resigned to the fact that there was little he could do since the damage was done. A few months later the couple came home and was shocked to find their basement full of water. They were extremely upset and called a different builder to come out to assess the damage and find some answers to their dilemma. The builder showed the couple the cracks in the foundation and stated the cracks in the bedrooms were the telltale signs of the house having foundation problems. The builder also informed the heartbroken couple that the ground in their area was not the best for a home. The couple was devastated by the news. After thinking back and reviewing the building process, they sheepishly acknowledged that their pride had gotten in the way. They did not adequately review the area to find the best ground for their home. They realized their home structure needed a stronger foundation to make it secure.

Like the home this couple had problems with, your current circumstances and future have much to do with the foundation of your life. You have experienced difficulties in your daily life that may be the telltale signs of larger problems. You may feel like your foundation is cracking or sinking right from under your feet. You cannot stand on that shaky foundation built on the lies and unhealthy relationships from the past. You must stand on a solid foundation of truth found in a personal relationship with Jesus Christ. If you are holding on to the destructive messages that have been told to you, you are living on a deceptive foundation of self-destruction. You need to get off that destructive foundation and rebuild your life on the solid rock of truth with what God has done and says about you. God is the origin where your truth has always been, is now, and will always be in the future. Set your life free by praying for the truth to become known in your heart and mind. Rely on the following truths:

- God is truth. "I am the way and the truth and the life. No one comes to the Father except through me" (John 14:6).
- If you know God you will know the truth. "But he who listens to me will live in safety and be at ease, without fear of harm" (Proverbs 1:33).
- You are a child of God made in His image. "...for in the image of God has God made man" (Genesis 9:6).
- Know that God loves you. "How great is the love the Father has lavished on us, that we should be called children of God!" And that is what we are! (1 John 3:1).
- God is your hope. "Hope does not disappoint us, because God has poured out His love into our hearts by the Holy Spirit, whom He has given us" (Romans 5:5).

The truth about your past

Although the old saying, the truth hurts, still applies, there is a healing element that follows once you finally acknowledge the hurts of your past. However the events in the past influenced your life, you should acknowledge those events cannot be changed. Although the memories from the past will be with you the rest of your life, you can change how the hurtful emotional memories currently affect you. The emotions that are triggered in adulthood are often the emotional memories created in childhood. You do not need to let those hurts hang over you like a dark rain cloud or a ball and chain around your neck. You may be so accustomed to feeling as if you could not change your circumstances, you still believe you are helpless to change. You can change by deciding to find the truth about those hurts and acknowledge the destruction that has taken place as a result of those hurts.

The truth about your feelings

For years you may have been denied the ability to freely say what you feel or you have expressed your feelings and received hurtful responses. You have been treated with disrespect that has hindered you from knowing the truth about your feelings. Remember the following truths about your feelings:

- **You were freely given feelings to freely express them.** You may think like a person in my office who said, "I don't know what I'm feeling!" You don't know because you were not allowed how to feel. You have the ability to feel because God originally gave the feelings to you. It was the people in your life who destroyed your ability to express or recognize those feelings. You have the right to express what God gave to you. If you have pushed those feelings deep inside, you may start out having difficulty finding your feelings. With the help of others, begin using the techniques in this book.

- **You will be in control when you identify and express your feelings.** If you have lived (or currently live) in a home where hurtful feelings have made you feel out of control, your natural tendency would be to ignore and suppress those hurts to survive the situation to feel in control. If you continue to ignore the feelings that are triggered, the suppressed emotional energy will fester like a disease that is out of control. When you make the decision to identify and release hurts, you are letting go of the disease and taking back control of our life. Do not let how people treated (or treat) you get in the way of expressing yourself now. If you were hurt when feelings were expressed, remember that you are allowed to have an opinion. God gave you the right to respectfully say what is on your heart and mind.

- **You are allowed to be happy.** You have every right to enjoy the happy moments in life. When you have been feeling unhappy, depressed, guilty, fearful, or oppressed for many years, you become accustomed to living on the sad side of your Feelings Gauge. God wants you to enjoy each day of your life. However, with each self-doubt, self-judgment, and self-criticism, you are sabotaging any chances for good feelings. If you don't understand why you have become unhappy, use the techniques you have learned to explore, identify, and change how you feel.

- **Emotional buttons trigger emotional memories.** When an adult situation triggers your emotional buttons of overwhelming feelings, remember that the situation was the trigger and the feelings were from your past. As you take responsibility to find out what and why the emotional buttons were pushed, you will be free from the belief that someone else has control over your feelings.

Finding the truth about the destructive messages

The truth is, you have believed and felt these destructive messages of thought and feelings for so long, it is hard to believe anything else. For many of you, there will be an inner struggle to overcome the destructive messages. The shame nature may be so deep that it would be difficult to believe you are good enough, no matter how many times you are told the truth. To find the truth, your heart needs a cleansing of the lies. Find the inner truth about these destructive messages with the help of God, who will provide the truth. "Surely you desire truth in the inner parts; you teach me wisdom in the inmost place" (Psalm 51:6).

You have come to realize these destructive lies of self-judgment, abandonment, hurt, fear, and shame were created from unhealthy interactions with others. Without the truth, your adult responses will be limited to the childlike emotions that you have come to know so well. Unless you uncover the truth about these lies you have come to believe, you will be destined to suffer with these lies the rest of your life. The only way you can know the truth is to find it from the One who created the truth and gives the truth. "Then you will know the truth, and the truth will set you free" (John 8:32). To help you uncover the truth about your destructive message, find a quiet place and begin by praying the following steps (detailed in Chapter Ten):

- God, is there any unforgiveness in my life that I need to confess?
- God, help me find where I learned these childlike feelings.
- God, take away this feeling of ("name the feeling") and help me find the truth.
- God, help me respond differently to my feelings.

Tell yourself the truth

For years you have been telling yourself the same continuously playing negative messages that were started by past unhealthy relationships. Each day that you allow these negative messages to be said by your mouth or played in your mind, you are doing the very same emotionally abusive act that was done to you by others. If you did not like those messages and actions when they were done to you in the past, why are you still emotionally abusing yourself in the present? As a child you did not have a choice as to the type of treatment you received from caregivers. If you now have the freedom to make choices as an adult, why are you still choosing to abuse yourself? Up to now you have never known anything different. If you have always had this unhealthy belief deep inside that you were not good enough, you do not need to abuse yourself any more. You are good enough and you can take control over what you say and do to yourself. You need to stop the destructive messages by doing the following:

*   **Realize you are not to blame**. For years you may have believed and acted on the shame nature premises that you were to blame for circumstances in your life. In fact, you still may take the blame for more than fifty percent of circumstances in your life. In plain English, this is a big lie. The lie may have started generations ago and it is up to you to decide to stop the lies in your generation. Whatever the age of your children, you still have the chance to change the lies for the next generation.
*   **You are good enough because God made you that way!** "I praise you because I am fearfully and wonderfully made; your works are wonderful, I know that full well" (Psalm 139:14). You cannot allow the destructive messages to tell you lies about yourself any more. You are wonderfully made because God does not make mistakes. You were created good enough by God because you were made in the image of God. "So God created man in His own image, in the image of God He created him; male and female He created them" (Genesis 1:27). Since God is your maker, whenever you shame and disrespect yourself, you are insulting God.
*   **Stop listening to the lies**. You need to stop using any destructive messages of self-judgments, self-doubts, insults, put downs, and criticisms. Do not believe the lies that you hear from others. You do not get your identity from what other people say about you. The truth is, you get

your identity from what God has done for you and what God says about you.

- **Tell yourself the truth every day**. Every day you should say true statements that are healing messages. Your heart, mind, and soul need to be healed through repeating positive, uplifting, affirming words. Write encouraging Bible scriptures on paper, or write the following list down on small cards and place the cards around your house and place of work. Say these positive statements in the morning and at night.

I am good enough.
I am precious in God's sight.
I am made in God's image.
God forgives me.
I am a unique and wonderful person.
I am free to express the feelings that God gave me.
I do not need to listen to and believe the destructive messages I hear.
I can accept the good things that God has for me today.

- **Give the hurts away**. You are not alone with your hurts and feelings. Do not let how you feel about yourself, or how you feel about others get in the way of letting yourself give away the hurts. You do not deserve to hold on to lies that are not your fault. Do not let self-judgment, self-doubt, or lies get in the way of letting others come into your life. Pray (and seek out) that a friend, family, or professional will come into your life to help with the healing process. You need to give the hurts away through the steps in this book and through other activities such as prayer, writing out your feelings, and talking with a professional who is familiar with identifying and changing the original destructive messages and lies within you.

The truth about God's forgiveness

"You are a forgiving God, gracious and compassionate, slow to anger and abounding in love" (Nehemiah 9:17). The negative messages and shame nature create the belief you are somehow at fault for what has happened in your life. Do not let the lies and the deceptions of Satan take away the truths that God is a loving, forgiving, and compassionate God. God wants you to be secure in His forgiveness. God wants you to be secure in His forgiveness by knowing the following:

- **Through Jesus Christ you are forgiven.** "For God so loved the world that He gave His one and only Son, that whoever believes in Him shall not perish but have eternal life. For God did not send his Son into the world to condemn the world, but to save the world through Him. Whoever believes in Him is not condemned, but whoever does not believe stands condemned already because he has not believed in the name of God's one and only Son" (John 3:16-18). No matter what you have done or how bad you believe you are, God can forgive you.

- **There is no condemnation or judgment for those who believe in Jesus Christ.** For the Law of the Spirit of life in Christ Jesus has set you free from the law of sin and death (see Romans 8:1). God believes in you and does not judge you when you believe in Jesus Christ.

- **Jesus is waiting for you to accept Him into your heart as your personal Savior and friend.** If you do not have a personal relationship with Jesus Christ, He wants you to accept Him right now. Ask Jesus into your heart to be forgiven once and for all. To be forgiven, sincerely pray this prayer: "Dear God, I realize I need forgiveness. Forgive me of my sins and cleanse my heart. Come into my heart as the Lord of my life, through Jesus Christ I pray." Let another Christian or someone close to you know you prayed this prayer.

- **When you accept Jesus, you become a new person.** Realize that "Therefore, if anyone is in Christ, he is a new creation; the old has gone, the new has come" (2 Corinthians 5:17). You have the reassurance that you have been forgiven of the past and can celebrate your clean and redeemed heart, mind, and body. You have the promise of God that you are a new creation. God has done His part to forgive you. Now, you must do your part and forgive yourself. You must allow God to forgive you and do not sabotage what He has done by taking back the belief that you are not forgiven.

The truth about forgiving yourself and others

"When you stand praying, if you hold anything against anyone, forgive him, so that your Father in heaven may forgive you your sins" (Mark 11:25). The longer you choose to hold unforgiveness toward yourself and others, the longer you choose not to receive forgiveness from God and delay emotional healing of your heart and mind. How can God forgive you if you do not forgive others? You must do your share of forgiving yourself and others for God to do His share of forgiving you.

- **You are free to choose forgiveness.** For years you may have believed you were too bad of a person to have the right to forgive someone else. You believed a lie that needed to be stopped. You are good enough and when you accept Jesus Christ, you are a new creation. You can forgive anyone you choose, anytime you want.

- **You are free of guilt, blame, and shame.** For years you may have felt overwhelmed with guilt, blame, or shame for countless issues. God never intended you to be filled with these destructive and unhealthy feelings. You received these negative feelings when people in your life transferred those feelings over to you. You must take responsibility for your own actions, but you do not need to own someone else's transfer of negative unhealthy shame and guilt. Remember, God has already forgiven you for all of those issues. It is your turn to let go of this baggage by asking for forgiveness, forgiving yourself, and others.

- **You are free to ask for forgiveness whenever you need it.** There is no limit on the amount of forgiveness that needs to come from you or that can be received from God. God knows your intentions as you continue to try and let go of a sinful habit. If you fall back into the bad habit, God will forgive again. However, like any loving father, God expects you to take responsibility to get rid of the habit as you said you intended. If the habit is too strong to handle yourself, you must seek the help from others.

The truth about giving love and receiving love

The shame and hurt you received created a judgment that you are second rate, not good enough, and unworthy to be loved. You may silently think, "How can anyone love a loser like me?" or "I need to always try harder if I'm going to be accepted." These are some of the lies that keep you in bondage of judgment that undermines your ability to love yourself and be loved by others. Consequently, you do not like yourself and believe you do not deserve to feel love, affection, even compliments from others. If you have not learned about love and have not received it, you do not know enough about love to give it away. I often hear from a spouse how their mate "doesn't show love." It is hard to imagine what love is if you have never experienced it from those closest to you. You need to make a choice that you want to learn how to give and receive love. Do not listen to those inner lies that say you cannot love. "Let us love one another, for love comes from God. Everyone who loves has been born of God and knows God" (1 John 4:7).

- **God loves you in spite of how you feel about yourself.** Do not believe the lies you have felt and heard over the years about yourself. God loves you because He created you. In the same way, you will love your child no matter the mistakes they have made, your Heavenly Father loves you no matter what mistakes you have made. Your Heavenly Father wants to love you and He is waiting for you to accept His love.
- **You are good enough to love and be loved.** You are good enough because you are created in the image of God and loved because you are a child of God. He wants you to give love away as you receive it from God. "We love because He first loved us" (1 John 4:19).
- **Rediscover love.** You still have the capability to be loved. If the hurts overshadow the love within you, there is no reason why you cannot learn to love. Start to love by doing the following:

Go through the processes of forgiveness found in Chapter Ten.
Pray daily for God to help you discover love.
Read daily the scripture, 1 Corinthians, Chapter 13.
Explore the Bible scriptures and other literature on love.
Pray to open yourself to God's love.
Pray for opportunities to receive love and give love to others.
When love comes your way, ask the other person to help you accept it.
Seek professional counseling if necessary.

The truth about faith

Over the years you may have survived by only trusting in yourself. The more people hurt you over the years, the more you lost faith and trust in people. You may not believe there is enough faith left within you to battle inner hurts and make the changes in your life. There is no reason why you need to make any changes by yourself. The fact that you are reading this book means you are willing to step out in faith and trust the thoughts of someone to help you make a difference in your life. The Bible says all you need is faith the size of a small mustard seed to make something big happen. "...I tell you the truth, if you have faith as small as a mustard seed, you can say to this mountain, 'Move from here to there' and it will move. Nothing will be impossible for you" (Matthew 17:20). Remember; do not stand on the amount of faith you believe is within you. Stand on what God says you have and what He will give you in faith to begin the task of changing your life. "My message and my preaching were not with wise and persuasive words, but with a demonstration of the Spirit's power, so that your faith might not rest on men's wisdom, but on God's power" (1 Corinthians 2:4-5).

The truth about hope for the future

Do not use your past to create your beliefs for the present; and do not let your present beliefs create your hopes of the future. Your hope for better days does not rest in the past or what you can accomplish in the future. Your hope only rests in your acceptance of what God has already done for you and your belief in what He has in store for you. "Hope does not disappoint us, because God has poured out His love into our hearts by the Holy Spirit, whom He has given us" (Romans 5:5).

Your future looks bright because you have decided to help yourself get this far. The next step is to put what you have learned into practice. You are recommended to have others help you make the changes in your life. The self-destructive lies you have thought and felt for years have been like a heavy chain wrapped around you. Over the years, the destructive links of that chain have been squeezing the life out of your heart, mind, and soul. You have tried breaking the chain with little success. If you try to make the changes alone, you will continue to struggle as you have in the past. To break the chain of shame, self-judgment, self-doubt, unforgiveness, and oppression you need a power mightier than yourself. There is no reason why you need to struggle and suffer any longer. Let the supernatural power of Almighty God help you break the destructive bondage to the hurts of the past to find glorious freedom in what you think and feel in the present and future.

Selected Bibliography

Bradshaw, John. *Healing the Shame That Binds You.* Florida: Health Communications, Inc., 1988.

Dobson, James, PhD. *Emotions can you trust them.* California: Regal Books, 1980.

Dodson, Fitzhugh, PhD and Alexander, Ann, MD. *Your Child: Birth to Age 6.* New York: Simon & Schuster, 1986.

Dufty, William. *Sugar Blues.* New York: Warner Books, 1975.

Kagan, Jerome. "How we become who we are." *Family Therapy Networker.* September/October, 1998.

Minirth, Frank, MD, and Meier, Paul, MD. *Counseling and the Nature of Man.* Michigan: Baker Books, 1982.

Minirth, Meier, Hemfelt, Sneed and Hawkins. *Love Hunger.* Nashville: Ballantine Books, 1990.

Pelletier, Kenneth. *Mind as Healer Mind as Slayer.* New York: Dell Publishing, 1977.

Pshelov, Steven, MD, Editor in Chief, and Hannemann, Robert MD. *Caring for your baby and young child, Age 5 to 12.* New York: Bantam Books, 1995.

Siegel, Bernie S., MD. *Peace, Love and Healing.* New York: Harper & Row, 1989.

Smith, Edward M, PhD. *Beyond Tolerable Recovery.* Kentucky. Althia Publishers, 1996.

Unger, Merrill F, PhD. *What Demons can do to Saints.* Illinois: Moody Press, 1991.

VanVonderen, Jeff. *Tired of Trying To Measure Up.* Minnesota: Bethany House Publishers, 1989.